COMPETENCE-BASED
EMPLOYMENT
INTERVIEWING

D0169139

COMPETENCE-BASED EMPLOYMENT INTERVIEWING

Jeffrey A. Berman

QUORUM BOOKS
Westport, Connecticut • London

Library of Congress Cataloging-in-Publication Data

Berman, Jeffrey A., 1942–
    Competence-based employment interviewing / Jeffrey A. Berman.
      p.   cm.
    Includes bibliographical references and indexes.
    ISBN 1–56720–050–8 (alk. paper)
    1. Employment interviewing. I. Title
    HF5549.5.I6B469   1997
    658.3'1124—dc21   96–54287

British Library Cataloguing in Publication Data is available.

Library of Congress Catalog Card Number: 96–54287
ISBN: 1–56720–050–8

First published in 1997

Quorum Books, 88 Post Road West, Westport, CT 06881
An imprint of Greenwood Publishing Group, Inc.

Printed in the United States of America

The paper used in this book complies with the
Permanent Paper Standard issued by the National
Information Standards Organization (Z39.48–1984).

10 9 8 7 6 5 4 3 2 1

Contents

Illustrations

Preface

This book is designed to provide a practitioner-oriented approach to competence-based employment interviewing. Since this form of interviewing is technical, the reader is provided with a theoretical framework which guides the process. If the interview is conducted skillfully, the job applicant will not be self-conscious when his/her background is being rigorously examined. The interview retains its function as a welcome to an outsider into the organization. Also, this book provides useful information on interviewing skills which can be used in many human resource management-related functions.

In writing this book I have received the help of numerous colleagues and friends. I acknowledge my colleague, John Murray III, who introduced me to this topic. I received support for the writing of this book from Salem State College, which provided me a research assistant. Josephat Mwangi, my research assistant, was very helpful to me in the final revision of the manuscript. The manuscript was reviewed by three colleagues, namely, Baruch Nevo, Natalie Miller, and Theodore Hansen. Their comments were very helpful. I would like to thank my wife, Beth Luchner, for designing the graphic material in the book.

I hope this book will be helpful to all who wish to make the employment interview a fair, objective, and practical means of selecting employees for their organization.

Part I

Introduction

Chapter One

Competence-Based Structured Interviewing Process

A number of trends have converged to improve the employment interview. The most recent trend is the emergence of competence as a foundation for human resource management. The emphasis on competence by human resource management practitioners has placed the structured interview at center stage in employee selection. While this technique is more complex than the traditional interview, it has gained acceptance because its impressive results tie into the strategic plans of many firms. Another important trend is the development of new research methodologies, which has thrown more light onto the effectiveness of the structured interview. Finally, there is the issue of equal employment opportunity. The selection process and the content of the employment interview is regulated by Federal and state laws in the United States. The compliance efforts of U.S. organizations have also led them to an increased level of sophistication in human resource management. The structured interview is now more feasible to implement in business settings.

The structured employment interview has been an established selection procedure for a long time. It has been estimated that thirty-two percent of employment interviews in the United States are structured to some extent (ASPA, 1983). However, there has been a great deal of resistance to this approach on the part of managers and employment interviewers (Dipboye, 1994). In fact, some proponents of this method propose very strict guidelines for interviews, which make it unlikely that most managers will adopt these procedures. On the other hand, it is possible to introduce more structure into employment interviewing while still assuring that the process will be acceptable to managers and interviewers.

Nevo and Berman (1994) examine the pros and cons of the structured versus the nonstructured interview. The nonstructured interview is described as being, in its purest form, an open-ended, individualized, conversational dialogue between the employer and the applicant. The structured interview is a formal question and answer session in which the employer assesses the applicant's specific qualifications in a predesigned, organized manner.

According to Nevo and Berman (1994), the unstructured employment interview is probably the most commonly used selection tool in North America and Western Europe and the sole selection device in many other countries. It has long been popular for several reasons. The employer can ask questions that go beyond a review of the applicant's resumé and credentials and can obtain a personal feel for whether or not the applicant would be suitable for the position and would fit into the social context of the company. The traditional employment interview is easy to administer, is face valid (accepted by applicants as a valid method of hiring), and is useful for recruiting, screening, final selection, and providing information to the applicant. Some of the major problems with the traditional interview are the following:

- Material is not covered consistently in traditional interviews.
- Interview validity is low.
- The attitude of the interviewer effects the interpretation of interviewees' responses.
- Interviewers are influenced more by unfavorable than favorable information. This is referred to as a negativity bias (Dipboye, 1992).
- Interviewers often reach a final decision early in the interview, typically within the first four minutes. This is known as a tendency to rush to judgment.
- Early impressions are more important than factual information in determining interviewers' judgments.
- After interviewers form a favorable impression, they spend more time talking than the interviewee.
- Research on bias in the interview clearly highlights that race, gender, and handicaps of applicants influence interview decisions.

The structured interview has emerged as a solution to these problems because it combines the features of the traditional interview with the features of a standardized selection procedure. Nevo and Berman (1994) identify five key aspects of the structured interview. Structure varies, and only a highly structured interview will emphasize all five features. They are the following:

- Specific dimensions to be covered in the interview are identified by job analysis.
- For every dimension, a pool of predetermined questions is prepared. Questions during the interview are taken from this pool.
- Rating is systematic. It is based on rating codes, anchored examples, and illustrations.
- The administration of the interview and its physical setting are standardized.

- A panel interview is desirable but not essential to assure reliability of the ratings.
- Training of interviewers is essential.

Nevo and Berman (1994) also identified problems with the structured interview. Structuring the interview may have a sterilizing effect on the procedure. The interview becomes less spontaneous and the interviewer may lose track of potentially important follow-up information. Another dehumanizing effect is the cold atmosphere that results from structuring. This effect may influence interviewees to be less open during the interview, and it may discourage applicants from pursuing employment with an impersonal organization, even if it is offered to them at a later stage. Interviewers and applicants tend to value an atmosphere where they can be spontaneous and direct. Also, the introduction of structure brings an opportunity for applicants to beat the system. The use of standard questions and a fixed-response rating code in the structured interview can be dangerous because lists of interview questions can be widely circulated. To counter this problem, Nevo and Berman suggest that the structured portion of the interview may be followed by a clinical interview under certain conditions. If the interviewer is trained in clinical interviewing, a clinical interview can be used to evaluate the applicant's mental health, personality, interpersonal skills, and stress tolerance. This procedure is not recommended for interviewers who do not have the appropriate training. An advantage of the clinical interview is that it allows the interviewer to follow up on clues provided by the applicant.

EQUAL EMPLOYMENT OPPORTUNITY

A problem with employment interviews from the standpoint of equal employment opportunity (EEO) is their subjectivity. According to Campion and Arvey (1989), when interviewers are not given clear guidelines for evaluating a candidate, subjectivity guides the process and provides a ready mechanism for illegal discrimination. The employment interview methodology suggested in this book is designed to be in conformity with the EEO Guidelines of the U.S. Equal Employment Opportunity Commission.

Many states have their own specific guidelines about employment interviewing. The reader should obtain a copy of those regulations in order to have a complete picture.

While there are some important prohibitions which constrain interviewers, the position of this book is that an employer can conduct a rigorous interview with any applicant and still respect the EEO guidelines.

RESEARCH ON EMPLOYMENT INTERVIEWING

In the domain of research on employment interviewing, there have been some significant recent developments. *Meta-analysis,* a statistical technique for combining the results of numerous related studies, has shown that a structured interview, when compared with the traditional (nonstructured) interview, is a powerful selection procedure. The traditional interview has long been criticized by researchers as being nonvalid as a predictor of subsequent job performance. The point of view of researchers is that the employment process is ideally a selection process. There should be a reasonable number of applicants for any position, and the task of the interviewer is to choose the applicant most likely to succeed on the job and in the organization. The process is nullified if there are too few applicants, if bias or favoritism plays a role, or if the selection procedures utilized are not rigorous.

A MODEL FOR THE SELECTION PROCESS

Competence-based employment interviewing proceeds according to very modern ideas about organizations. The traditional view of organization is built around the concept of a job for which the best qualified individual is selected. This works well in a traditional organization. Today the model for organization is based on open communication and participation of all members. Team effort, as opposed to the individual contributor, is now a cultural norm. There is no longer a prescribed career path which permits one to rise in the organization through a well-defined set of jobs. In fact, an employee knows that he/she may work for several organizations during a career.

In order to deal with this complexity, the concept of competence has come to the fore. An applicant or employee can be assessed to ascertain his/her competence on employment related factors. In the past a job description was the basic source document for ascertaining what dimensions (e.g., tasks, skills, knowledge, and abilities) were job related. Now an employee may be expected to perform a wide range of roles as a member of a team. Furthermore, their present roles may be changed or eliminated in order to reposition the organization to implement a new strategy. Role description has replaced job description in many organizations. By adopting the concept of competence, the human resource management function has the means to deal with changes. The competent employee will be able to perform the present job and will be able to take on changes in work as they occur.

A comprehensive model is the foundation of the interviewing process recommended in this book. It is entitled, Competence-Based Structured Interviewing Process. The model is illustrated in Figure 1.1. The interviewing process is envisaged to have the following important components: preparation for the interview, interviewing techniques, and evaluation of applicants. This is a brief overview of the model. A thorough explanation of each aspect of the model is contained in Part II.

The first step in the preparation process is the analysis of the open position. A basic premise of employment interviewing at this time is that the entire process should be job related. In order to assure that the process is job related,

Figure 1.1
Competence-Based Structured Interviewing Process

Preparation for the Interview

Position Analysis	Competence Factors	Question Development
Critical Incidents	Competence A	Job Knowledge Questions
and/or	Competence B	Behavior Description Questions
Job Analysis: Tasks	Competence C	Behavioral Intention Questions
• Skills	Competence D	Worker Requirement Questions
• Knowledge	Competence n	
• Abilities		

Interviewing Techniques

Develop Rapport

•

Obtain Answers to Structured Questions

Use Good Interview Technique

Take Notes

•

Present Desired Image of Organization

•

Consistent Approach to All Applicants

Evaluation of Applicants

Evaluation Rating Form	Evaluation Worksheet	Final Selection Decision
Competence A 1 2 3 4 5	Compare Scores of Multiple Interviewers	❑ Hire
Competence B 1 2 3 4 5		❑ Do not hire
Competence n 1 2 3 4 5		
Summary Rating 1 2 3 4 5		

a position analysis is conducted prior to the interview. Many organizations already have relevant information in their human resource information systems. However, due to the rapid changes in job content in many organizations, it will be necessary to update such information. The interviewer will place the emphasis on defining what competences are needed to perform the job.

Two approaches are suggested in order to ascertain information about competence. The *critical incident technique* is used to develop information about the performance of highly successful job incumbents. It is believed that people who are highly successful in a job have developed the most efficient means of doing the job. Therefore it is necessary to analyze the job performance of these highly successful individuals, and the critical incident technique is a proven technique for doing so.

Critical incidents related to job success are analyzed to ascertain the competences of individuals which have led to their success. The *job analysis technique* is also used to analyze open positions. Typically the job analysis technique focuses on all job incumbents, and the information it yields on competence is couched in terms of tasks performed and skills, knowledge, and ability. Competence must then be inferred from this information.

Competence factors are the basic elements of the process. Each open job is characterized by the competence factors needed to achieve successful (and highly successful) performance. Examples of such factors are the following: planning and organizing ability, decisiveness, analytical skills, leadership ability, sensitivity, communication skills, and so forth. The goal of the interview is to obtain information on a candidate's standing on each of the relevant competences. In order to do so, a set of questions is developed prior to the interview. A process of question development yields the following types of questions: job knowledge questions, behavior description questions, situational questions, and questions about whether a worker has the required qualifications for a job.

The next part of the model covers the interview process. This is the aspect of the model with which most practitioners are familiar. There is a traditional form of the employment interview which covers in chronological order many topics, such as educational background, work experience, interests and outside work activities, and motivation. In the structured interview, the format of the interview is different. The interviewer asks the same questions of each applicant. In a highly structured interview, the questions are asked in the same order and in the same way for each applicant. The main issues in conducting an interview are the following: develop rapport with the applicant; obtain answers to structured questions; use good interview technique; take notes; present the desired image of the organization; and make sure that the interview is consistent for all applicants.

The final part of the process is the evaluation of applicants. The key to evaluation is rating the applicant on the same job-related factors which formed the basis for interview questions. A rating scale with numerical anchors, as pictured in the model, is used to rate the applicant on each factor. The interviewer uses behavioral information obtained in the interview to make each rating. The interviewer should be able to document ratings from notes taken during and after the interview. A summary rating on the applicant's overall competence can also be made. It may be necessary for multiple interviews to be consolidated into a single rating for each applicant. This rating is then input into the final decision process leading to a hiring decision.

OVERVIEW OF THE BOOK

In Chapter 2, Competence as the Basis for Human Resource Management Systems, the competence movement in human resource management is reviewed. By looking at competence as a guiding force in all aspects of human resource management, the role of competence in employment interviewing will be more clear.

Part II deals with the how-to aspect of the competence-based structured interviewing process. Chapter 3, Preparation for the Interview, deals with the issues preceding the actual interview. Suggestions for conducting a critical incident-based position analysis are featured. Before an interview can take place, the position must be analyzed to determine its tasks and the skills, knowledge, and abilities required to perform the tasks. Techniques for performing this analysis are contained in Chapter 3. Examples of the question development process are provided. The recommended structure for an interview is another key topic of Chapter 3. A case study is used to provide graphic examples which can serve as the basis for the reader's own application of the principles embodied in the book.

When one is in contact with a job applicant a wide range of interpersonal communication skills come into play. Chapter 4, Interviewing Techniques, is designed to provide information on interviewing skills. Many details specifically concerning the employment interview are covered. The approach is both technical and practical. Some aspects of the traditional employment interview can be retained in the structured interview approach. It is recognized that the employment interview is used not only for selection but also to encourage candidates to remain in competition for the open position. The case study is extended into Chapter 4 in order to provide an example of the structured interview.

Chapter 5, Evaluation of Applicants, shows the reader how to take the information received from the candidate and to proceed to a decision. The candidate must be evaluated on the same job-related basis which is used to form the questions used in the interview. Anticipated applicant responses obtained in the preparation phase are useful in documenting the ratings made for each applicant. A rating should be documented by an incident which illustrates how the applicant has performed in the past in a work or educational setting.

Incidents which the applicant relates to the interviewer which coincide with critical incidents needed for successful job performance are the best predictors of future job success (Janz, 1989). The case study is continued in Chapter 5, and evaluation of the candidate in the case is provided. Also, examples of rating instruments are provided. The reader can generate a complete competence-based structured interview procedure using the material in Chapters 3, 4, and 5. This book serves as a reference for the development of procedures which meet the specific needs of an organization.

Part III of the book deals with EEO. An emphasis of the book is on fair employment practices. Employment interviewing is covered by the Uniform Guidelines on Employee Selection published by the U.S. Equal Employment Opportunity Commission. There are numerous state guidelines on employment interviewing in the United States. Chapter 6, Equal Employment Opportunity and the Employment Interview, covers the basics of these regulations. An interviewer is shown how to proceed with the process of a rigorous interview while adhering to regulations.

Part IV of the book deals with research on employment interviewing. Research is important since advances in interviewing have come from the community of personnel researchers. Part IV opens with Chapter 7, which highlights results from previous reviews of the literature on employment interviewing research. Periodically a scholar will review research on employment interviewing and its implications for practitioners. One can learn much from these summaries of research findings. The results of past reviews also establish the agenda for topics which need additional study. Chapter 8 deals with the issue of panel interviews. Chapter 9 focuses on the various approaches to structured employment interviewing which have been documented in the research literature. The topic of Chapter 10 is the validity of the employment interview. In order to follow the discussion of statistical methods in Chapter 10, a knowledge of basic statistics is needed. Practitioners who want to fully understand this discussion can refer to basic texts on statistics and industrial/organizational psychology for relevant background information.

Chapter Two

Competence as the Basis for Human Resource Management Systems

While competence has long been a standard in employee selection, a recent trend in human resource management (HRM) has led to the introduction of competence into many aspects of employment decision making. The definition of competence accepted by most HRM practitioners in the United States was expressed by Richard Boyatzis in his 1982 book, *The Competent Manager*. He defined competence as any personal trait, characteristic, or skill which can be shown to be directly linked to effective or outstanding job performance. A more general definition, which can be applied to any occupation, is provided by Spenser and Spenser (1993). They define a competence as an underlying characteristic of an individual that is causally related to criterion referenced effective or superior performance in a job or situation. They believe competence indicates a way of behaving or thinking, a way of generalizing across situations, and that competence endures for a reasonably long period of time. They cite five types of competence, namely, motives, traits, self-concept, knowledge, and skill. They believe that competence always includes an intent, which is the motive or trait force that causes action toward an outcome. They believe that in complex jobs (e.g., high-level technical positions, marketing positions, professional positions, and managerial positions) competence is relatively more important in predicting superior performance than are task-related skills, intelligence, or credentials. They believe that what distinguishes superior performers in these jobs is motivation, interpersonal skills, and political skills, all of which are competences.

Competence is a concept that can be applied to all categories of employees. A broad definition of competence is offered by the consulting firm of Towers Perrin (O'Neal and White, 1994). It defines competence as a combination of skills, knowledge, and behaviors that is important for the success of the organization, personal performance, and enhanced contribution. The firm defines two categories of competences, namely, enabling competence and domain competence. Enabling competence is essential for the business to achieve its strategy, is typically behavioral in nature, and is generally relevant to all employees. Domain competence is required for success in a particular job family and typically involves demonstrating technical/expert knowledge in a profession, occupation, vocation, field of study, or process area.

Another definition of competence in the United States focuses specifically on managers. Sternberg and Wagner (1991) identify a trait they call tacit knowledge. Tacit knowledge is the academic term for street smarts, a talent for learning the kind of practical knowledge that can only be acquired through experience. It is said to be what one needs to know to get ahead that is not specifically taught. It is not a measure of intelligence quotient (IQ). Sternberg and Wagner have developed the Tacit Knowledge Inventory for Managers to assess tacit knowledge. The inventory has been validated, and it distinguishes between successful and unsuccessful managers. This interesting development should not be considered as the discovery of a single factor that would lead to the prediction of managerial competence and success. According to Sternberg and Wagner, a high score on a test of tacit knowledge does not measure whether a person will act on that knowledge, or even whether a person is able to act on that knowledge.

In the United States, there have been competence-based programs in business organizations for over twenty years. The assessment center method, skill-based pay, and structured employment interviewing have been practiced by many organizations. Each of these methods has impressive scientific documentation of the impact of the program on performance outcomes. However, the increased emphasis on competence being tied to the strategic plans of organizations has spawned a new generation of competence-based HRM programs.

CASE STUDIES OF STRUCTURED
INTERVIEW PROGRAMS

Examples of how competence-based structured interviewing have saved companies money abound. Bell (1992) states that highly structured interviews are in use at AT&T, Scott Paper, Hershey Corporation, and many government agencies. Church (1996) reports that structured interviews or patterned interviews are used at Procter & Gamble, First Union Bank, and Coopers and Lybrand CPAs. Taylor and O'Driscoll (1995) report that Harman Management, the largest franchisee of Kentucky Fried Chicken in the United States, has estimated that it has achieved a $9,500,000 increase in sales volume and a $1,240,000 cost savings in reduced staff turnover through using structured interviews. Lunn (1993) reports that brewers Joshua Tetley in England have noted significant increases in profits over a five-year period as a result of selecting top performing managers through structured interviews. Cascio (1992) reports that J.C. Penney Company estimates it has received a $10 million payoff over two and one-half years by adopting a structured interview approach.

An organization which has used this technique to improve its management is the Digital Equipment Corporation (DEC) (Ennis and Lawson, 1995). DEC was faced with a massive downsizing (60,000 employees laid off) and reorientation of its strategy, from being an organization with a technologically based culture to a market-driven culture. Consequently, DEC created many new jobs based on the required competences for implementing the new strategy. Candidates for the new jobs could be current employees or new employees. Each candidate had to take a structured interview in which he/she related critical incidents from their work experience that they saw as relevant to the new position. The critical incidents were then analyzed by trained assessors, and an evaluation of the candidate was done. By means of this restructuring at the position level, DEC ensured that people with the necessary competence were in place to implement the new strategy the company created in order to reposition itself. The fact that the company was losing huge amounts of money and its very survival was threatened at the time served to heighten the importance of this movement toward competence-based employee selection procedures and permitted the use of more rigor in selection than had been possible in the past.

Van Clieaf (1991) provides an example of how a structured interview was used in a search for a director of international tax planning in a corporation.

The vice president of Finance expects the six person Tax Department to save the corporation at least $10 million a year in tax liability. The client conservatively estimated the amount that both the highly competent and the average international tax director could save the corporation in each of the first three years. The net present value of estimated tax savings for the average international tax director was $3.5 million, as compared to the highly competent tax director at $7 million . . . . The ability to identify, differentiate, and attract the highly competent international tax director versus the average tax director would have measurable impact on the bottom line. (317)

The results of competence modeling are used to establish the questions to be asked in the interview at this firm.

The highly structured interview has generated well-documented results. Campion, Pursell, and Brown (1988) report on a project in a large paper mill located in the rural southeast of the United States. The interview was used to hire entry-level labor-pool employees in a unionized environment. The company sought to employ people with the basic skills needed to perform any of seventeen entry-level jobs which could become available. A standardized interview of twenty questions, which lasted thirty minutes, was developed. The interview was administered to job applicants by a three-person panel. A total of 393 new employees were hired during the test phase of the project. A concurrent validation study was carried out using performance measures which were rated by supervisors. The structured interview improved the success rate of hiring new employees from fifty-five percent (traditional interview) to seventy percent (structured interview).

COMPETENCE-BASED HRM PROGRAMS

Perhaps the most dramatic application of the competence concept to HRM are the company-wide efforts. Some of these projects occur in green fields situations (i.e., opportunities for the development of new HRM practices) such as a new manufacturing plant. Others occur in mature businesses which are seeking to align HRM with their corporate strategic planning. An example of the green fields approach is provided by the Consumer Products Division of the Walt Disney Company (Cava, 1995). In this division, rapid growth (from 200 to 20,000 employees and from $100 million to $2.5 billion in revenue) occasioned the decision to introduce a competence-based HRM system. In the Consumer Products Division, competence is defined as a constellation of knowledge, skills, and motivations clustered to provide a description of the complex job of managing and leading. HRM subsystems have been developed based on this definition of competence and include the following: structured interviews for employee selection; 360 degree performance management for performance evaluation; tie-in between performance management results and pay raises; assessment centers for employee development; and custom-designed management training programs matrixed against strategic core competences. Each of these subsystems has been implemented, and the human resource director is planning to evaluate the competence-based practices to determine the impact of the competence model on organizational outcomes.

Another large organization which has implemented a total HRM system based on the competence model is Colgate-Palmolive. The effort at Colgate-Palmolive is global in scope. Competence is defined as the critical knowledge, skills, and behaviors defined for key positions in the organization which ensure a common understanding of what is required for performance excellence around the Colgate world (Smith, 1995). A competence model was developed for Colgate-Palmolive managers worldwide. There is a direct tie-in between the company's business strategy and its HRM system. In the staffing function, competence defines the job skills for the staffing process, prompts targeted questions in the interview guide, and is a critical basis of selection (competence-based interviews) and assessment (assessment center) decisions. In the performance management function, competence is focused both on results (what) and on the assessment of performance against objectives (how) in order to begin the identification of development needs. In the development planning function, the focus is on the identification and development of competences which support the achievement of organization and individual effectiveness. Colgate-Palmolive managers worldwide receive individual development plans as the result of this process. In the education and training function, the curriculum aims to build competence required at specific levels and by functional area in order to meet changing business needs and to foster continuous learning. In the succession planning function, competence is used to identify skill gaps as well as individuals who could potentially assume key organizational roles. The Colgate-Palmolive system was implemented in an organization with already established practices. This is a complex undertaking requiring a change of methodology as well as of a competence model.

CONCLUSIONS

In the United States at present, the concept of competence is at the center of attention in HRM. The concept of strategic planning explains a large part of this phenomenon. In the theory of strategic planning, the concept of competence plays a large part. Organizations are counseled to identify their core competences and their unique competences. Among other things, it is these competences which permit the organization to compete and win against its competition. A successful strategy will focus on an organization's existing competence or will require that the organization develop the required competence in order to implement the strategy. A major problem in strategic planning is that once organizations have gone to great expense to develop a winning strategy, many times the failure is one of implementation. The organization lacks the human resources, the culture, or the structure and systems necessary to support the strategy. The elevation of competence as a priority in HRM can be seen as an attempt to address this aspect of the dilemma of implementing strategy. Organizations are now aligning their human resource systems with their strategic plans. Competence profiles are the foundation for programs in staffing (internal and external), performance management, career development, succession planning, training and development, team formation and development, and human resource planning (Mirabile, 1994). As the result of this high level of activity, there are the beginnings of a scientific record of the validity of the competence concept as a predictor of success in management. Another trend that has influenced the ascendence of competence is competition. As markets become more efficient, competition intensifies. In many industries, automation, downsizing, and globalization have already been used to meet competition. Often what remains is to make better use of human resources. Competence provides a performance-based standard that can become the center of a HRM system.

Structured interviewing is one of several programs which are being used to implement competence-based HRM. While it is desirable to have a unified HRM system based on competence, it is possible to have a stand-alone interviewing program as well. This book focuses exclusively on employment interviewing, but it is important to consider the interview in the context of the entire HRM function.

A NOTE ON DEFINITIONS

In writing this book, the author uses only the terms *competence* and *competences*. The reader should be aware that some HRM practitioners use the terms *competency* and *competencies*, as opposed to competence and competences. Although they are equivalent terms according to the dictionary, for these practitioners the terms have different meanings. For these HRM practitioners, *competency* and *competencies* imply a way of understanding and identifying exceptional performance by individuals that focuses on either behaviors alone or a combination of behaviors and functional skills. By contrast, *competence* and *competences* denote ways of listing the aspects of purely acceptable performance, based on observable functional skills. While these distinctions have relevance for some aspects of HRM (e.g., management development and performance management), they are less relevant with regard to employment interviewing. In the employment interviewing process, it is the practice of having a sufficient applicant pool and choosing the best applicant from that pool, which makes it possible for excellent performance on the part of the new employee to be predicted. The process of employee selection is a system. Hence the system model used throughout the book. The employment interview is an aspect of that system. The interview can be effective only if sufficient applicants are available. Otherwise, pragmatic considerations such as filling a position in a timely manner will override the goal of making a good selection decision. In some programs (e.g., hiring leading graduates of universities for fast-track positions in blue-chip companies), competence and excellence are inextricably linked; and the employer will make no compromise on selecting the best candidate. However, if hiring must be a pragmatic matter based on labor-market conditions, the selection criterion will be filling open positions with qualified applicants. In these circumstances, the criterion is defined as meeting the requirements of the position description in order to permit the organization to meet its operating requirements.

Part II

Methodology of Structured Interviews

Chapter Three

Preparation for the Interview

An employment interview is based on thorough preparation by the interviewer. If the interviewer is not familiar with the open position and if a current position description is not available, the preparation time requires a significant effort. Too often, the reality is that the interviewer takes very little, if any, time to prepare. The interviewer skims the resumé or application, and takes it from there. This approach reveals to the applicant the lack of preparation and sometimes leads to embarrassing mistakes.

The interviewing process advocated here is based on thorough preparation. It is also based on the assumption that the interviewer will be seeing several applicants for a job, and the interviewer's goal is to select the best qualified applicant. Therefore, preparation will yield an interview schedule which is aimed at getting the most information from each applicant, while being fair to all applicants. Each applicant deserves a thorough hearing.

A MODEL FOR THE PREPARATION PROCESS

In the model depicted in Figure 3.1, the preparation process is highlighted. The model highlights the emphasis on position analysis. Position analysis has always been the recommended foundation for employment interviewing. With the advent of government regulation of employee selection, position analysis was incorporated into the HRM systems of most large business organizations and government contractors. The job relevance of the hiring process, a major requirement of government EEO regulations, is maintained by basing inquiries to job applicants on job requirements which result from position analysis. In the competence-based structured interview procedure, the critical incident technique has emerged as the preferred way to do position

Figure 3.1
Competence-Based Structured Interviewing Process—Preparation for the Interview

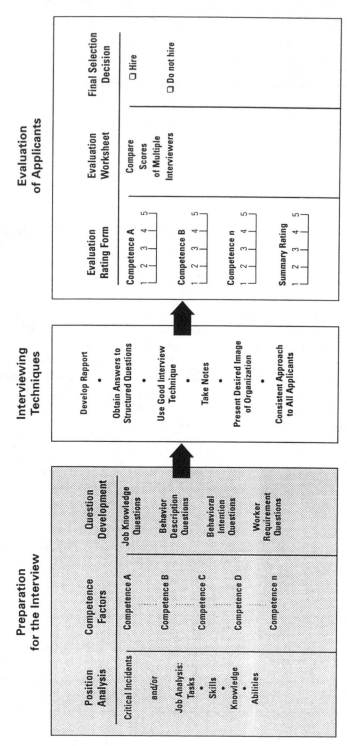

analysis. This is because it allows the interviewer to focus on the performance of highly competent job incumbents. The critical incident technique yields competence factors directly.

The traditional job analysis is also an effective way to prepare for the structured interview. Job analysis is another method used to do position analysis. If job analysis is used, competence factors may be developed as an additional step once the job analysis is complete. The competence-based structured interviewing model highlights the job analysis process whereby the interviewer moves from tasks, skills, knowledge, and abilities to the development of competence factors.

If a job analysis has not been conducted, it is up to the interviewer to obtain the information through a study of existing documents and interviews with job incumbents and supervisors.

The development of competence factors is the next step to be taken after a job analysis is performed. Once the interviewer understands the tasks, required experience, and personal characteristics needed to perform the job successfully, the interviewer may develop competence factors. Employee competence factors are behavioral descriptions which parallel task behaviors. Task behaviors are often very specific. If applicants are very experienced, the interviewer may be able to seek exact work experience in their background. Often, however, an employer will have applicants who have solid experience but who have not performed in a job exactly like the open job. Employee competence factors allow one to evaluate such applicants. In order to develop an employee competence factor, one takes a task and identifies an equivalent competence factor. In an employment interview an applicant may demonstrate varying degrees of a competence factor, namely, not much, some, an adequate amount, a lot, or superior competence.

A key aspect of employee competence factors is that they may be created for any job requirement. Since applicants will vary in the amount of an employee competence factor they possess, the employee competence factor is a good way of measuring the variation among applicants in job-related characteristics. Developing employee competence factors is a technique all employment interviewers should master. It is a form of abstract thinking, since employee competence factors are abstractions of actual job tasks, work activities, and requirements. Employee competence factors represent job tasks, work activities, and job requirements in behavioral terms. This is important because much of what applicants say will be in behavioral terms. By creating employee competence factors, the interviewer will be establishing a basis for evaluating applicants which will be in tandem with the information applicants will be giving to the interviewer.

The next phase of the competence-based structured interviewing model involves the development of questions. Up until now, the approach has been focused on the job opening. In order to utilize information about the open job, the interviewer must integrate it into the interview format. The interview is a question and answer session. The questions should be designed to obtain information from applicants relevant to the open job. The interviewing method suggested in this model involves the use of structured interview questions and probes. The structured interview question gives the applicant a chance to respond with information related to the job. The probe questions allow the interviewer to direct the interview to areas of direct relevance to the job opening.

In addition to structured interview and probe questions about an applicant's background, a set of questions about intended work behavior may be developed. Intended work behavior is useful information for the selection process. Such behavioral intentions give insight about the applicant's skills, knowledge, and abilities. While behavioral intentions are not direct measurement of skills, knowledge, and abilities, they represent a category of information which is just as important. The questions are constructed in a way that permits the applicants to express what they would do in a hypothetical situation.

CRITICAL INCIDENT TECHNIQUE

A popular method for determining desired employee competence is the critical incident technique. A *critical incident* involves a specific situation and the behavior which the job holder used to perform successfully in the situation. A classic description of how critical incidents of successful job incumbents were obtained is provided by Kirchner and Dunnette (1957). Kirchner and Dunnette describe the rationale of the critical incident technique.

Critical incidents are just what the name implies—occurrences that have proved to be the key to effective performance on the job. They involve not routine activities but rather those essentials in job performance which make the difference between success and failure. In applying the technique, critical incidents are recorded in the form of stories or anecdotes about how a person handles certain situations, and from these data a composite picture of job behavior is built up. (359)

In a study of salespeople at a large manufacturing firm, critical incident forms were sent to eighty-five sales managers in four separate product divisions. Each manager was asked to report as many critical incidents as possible illustrating both effective and ineffective behavior among his/her group of salespeople. The form asked the following questions:

Think back over a period of time (six months or so) long enough for you to have observed the activities of all your salespeople. Focus your attention on any one thing that one of your sales people may have done which made you think of him/her as an outstandingly good or very effective salesperson. In other words, think of a *critical incident* which has added materially to the overall success of your sales group. Respond to the following questions: What were the general circumstances leading up to this incident? Tell exactly what your sales person did that was so effective at the time. How did this particular incident contribute to the overall effectiveness of your sales group? When did this incident happen? How long has the salesperson been employed at your company? In the present territory? (Kirchner and Dunnette, 1957, 359)

A total of 135 incidents were reported, of which 96 could be classified as usable. Of these 96, 61 were instances of effective performance while 35 concerned non-effective performance. To illustrate the type of information contained in these reports, five of the incidents reported are given below (359):

1. A sales representative received notification from a customer about a defect in a product. The sales representative did not investigate the matter. Nor did the sales representative write up the complaint. Although the customer returned the defective product, no credit was issued to the customer. Although the customer continues to do business with the supplier, the customer is extremely dissatisfied.

2. A substantial customer was not satisfied with the product. The customer was in the process of trying out a substitute product from another supplier. The sales representative promised to develop an improved product in order to keep the business. Although the new product was developed and produced, the customer continued to receive the older version from a jobber who was trying to liquidate inventory. The customer lost confidence in the sales representative and closed the account.

3. A sales representative noticed a truck in the street carrying machines which required the use of raw materials he/she sold. The sales representative followed the truck to its destination. Later the sales representative called on the place where the machines were delivered. The sales representative was able to open a new account with this customer.

4. An account with a jobber was lost. A sales representative made regular in-person calls to the jobber. During these calls the benefits of his/her product lines were explained to the jobber. After a long period of time, the jobber resumed doing business with the company.

5. A large defense contractor ran out of product that had to be custom-made to specifications. The sales representative obtained raw materials from a jobber and arranged for them to be modified to the customer's specifications by a nearby workshop. The effort of the sales representative allowed the defense project to proceed until a new custom-made batch of product could be prepared for the customer.

Bell (1992) provides an example in an analysis of a sales position. "Problem: A client delayed placing an order because he had a technical product question that the salesperson could not answer on the spot. Successful behavior: salesperson validated client's question, promised to find the answer, and followed through in a timely way. Client proceeded with the purchase." (76)

The critical incidents discovered in the preparation process are the basis for determining the competence factors to be sought after in job applicants. While critical incidents may be descriptions of a situation which occurred, it is essential to translate them into behavioral terms. If this has not been provided by job holders or their supervisors, the interviewer must do so. A methodology for translating critical incidents into competence factors is provided.

METHODOLOGY OF THE CRITICAL INCIDENT TECHNIQUE

Taylor and O'Driscoll (1995) have described how the critical incident technique is used in preparing for a structured interview. They suggest that subject matter experts (SMEs) including supervisors, job incumbents, and any others who are familiar with the open position describe particularly effective and ineffective examples of actual past job performance. Such descriptions should be based on the experience of the SME or the experience of past or present holders of the position. Examples of critical incidents at the appropriate level of detail are provided earlier in this chapter.

In developing examples of critical incidents, three elements must be included, namely, the situation faced by the job incumbent, the job incumbent's behavior, and the outcome.

In order to be helpful, an SME must have experience with a position. A six-month minimum of experience is suggested by Taylor and O'Driscoll (1995). When there are few SMEs available, individual interviews are preferred. When more SMEs are available, small group interviews or questionnaires may be used.

In the questionnaire approach, the following elements are contained in the questionnaire: (1) the questionnaire may be designed to elicit critical incidents for the job as a whole, or it may be designed to elicit from each participant critical incidents from each main job task; (2) the job title of the position to be studied is stated at the outset; (3) each respondent is asked to think of three incidents of effective performance and three incidents of ineffective performance (these must be incidents which actually occurred); and (4) the anonymity of employees involved in the incidents is respected, and people are referred to by their job title only.

If the interview approach is used, the position analyst asks for as many critical incidents as can be remembered by each SME. Usually between five and twenty critical incidents may be elicited from each SME. The position analyst should seek to elicit a total of 100 critical incidents for each position. Finally, the SMEs group the critical incidents obtained into five to ten competences.

COMPETENCES AND CRITICAL INCIDENTS

Another process for determining which competences are necessary for a position has been developed by Van Clieaf (1991). The first step in the process is the identification of key performance measures for the position. This analysis yields the performance results wanted from holders of the position and the basis for establishing whether the performance results were accomplished. The second step in the process is to ascertain the work activities engaged in by the holder of the position in order to obtain successful performance. "Exemplary performers or managers of exemplary performers identify critical incidents in which an individual performed a key task and exhibited one or more of the performance dimensions. What the individual did, how he or she did it, and the results are all identified. Behavior is then ranked as ineffective, average, or exemplary, establishing an approximate behavior-based guide for rating performance" (317). The third step in the process is the identification of performance dimensions (i.e., competence factors) associated with the work activities identified in the critical incident analysis. The broad categories of performance dimensions Van Clieaf utilizes are the following: leadership skills, management skills, cognitive skills, interpersonal skills, communication skills, occupational knowledge, transition ability, motivation, and values. According to Van Clieaf, an important task is identifying and prioritizing the appropriate performance dimensions into two or three groups based on how critical the dimensions are to position effectiveness.

JOB ANALYSIS

In the event that an interviewer is unfamiliar with the open job, a job description is unavailable or out of date, or documentation is needed for the interview process, a job analysis can be conducted. The importance of job analysis in employment interviewing has long been recognized from the standpoint of HRM. There is also a legal basis to job analysis. The legal basis stems from the Uniform Guidelines for Employee Selection (EEOC, 1978). The Uniform Guidelines require that job analysis be performed as part of the development, application, and validation of employee selection procedures. For more information on the guidelines, see Chapter 6.

The points to keep in mind with regard to job analysis are the following:

- Some form of job analysis should be conducted prior to the employment interview. (The processs of job analysis and position analysis are oftentimes identical.)
- Data from the job analysis (a job description) should be used to develop interview questions and rating scales.
- Even if there were no legal pressures to conduct job analysis it should be done anyway. (Job analysis is the most sound basis for developing HRM selection procedures.)

JOB ANALYSIS METHODOLOGY

A job analysis is the first step in the competence-based structured interview process. The job analysis establishes the job relatedness of subsequent steps in the selection procedure. The job analysis provides key information for the interviewing process.

Arvey and Faley (1988) summarize the most common techniques for conducting a job analysis as follows: (1) interviewing individuals familiar with the job (e.g., job holders, supervisors, and SMEs); (2) observe the job being performed; (3) surveying individuals familiar with the job by using a questionnaire; and (4) review existing information (e.g., the Dictionary of Occupational Titles, prior job analysis reports, a prior job description, procedure manuals, training manuals and related materials, scheduling requirements, travel requirements, salary data, and laws and regulations which job holders must enforce).

Taylor and O'Driscoll (1995) state that SMEs can be asked to list tasks for a particular job. Alternatively, the SME is asked to amend a task list developed by a job analyst who has used job descriptions, training manuals, the Dictionary of Occupational Titles, or other reference materials. The SME is often asked to rate the importance of each task and its frequency of performance. This information is useful in weighting competences for use in subsequent analyses.

The U.S. Department of Labor (1972) makes the following recommendations about interviewing job incumbents: (1) the job analyst should first become familiar with the technologies of the job; (2) the job analyst should be versed in how to conduct a job analysis interview (for details consult a human resource management textbook); and (3) take notes during the interview.

DEVELOPING COMPETENCE FACTORS
FROM JOB ANALYSIS DATA

One of the most important techniques which an employment interviewer must develop is the identification of employee competence factors in a job. Sometimes an employee competence is obvious. For example, a word processor must have a specified skill level. It is often expressed in words per minute without errors. This competence is clearly job related and can also be easily measured. Many job competences are less easy to define and measure, but it is necessary to devote an effort to the process of identifying such competences. There is a knack to identifying employee competence. It is a form of inference. One starts with a job characteristic, namely, a task, a responsibility, a duty, a condition, or a standard of performance. From the job characteristic, one infers an aspect of the employee, which would assure fulfillment of the job characteristic. There is no guarantee that the new employee will be able to perform according to the standards. However, if one finds an applicant who has demonstrated competence which relates to job demands, one can predict this employee will be successful.

Job characteristics are mechanistic. Employee competence factors are organic. Making the transition from mechanistic to organic is not easy. It requires understanding on the part of the interviewer. It also requires a process whereby job characteristics are translated into employee competence factors. With some effort, every aspect of job performance can be translated into a behaviorally based competence factor. People are willing to disclose their work-related behavior in job analysis interviews. This is the major challenge to every employment interviewer. One must translate work activities into behaviors manifested by workers as they perform their job. Such behaviors are relatively easy to obtain from interviewees and can easily be measured (rated) for the purpose of employee selection.

Taylor and O'Driscoll (1995) state that in order to infer competences from tasks, the end results of the job, accountabilities, accomplishments, or job outputs must be identified. Each end result is broken down into its component tasks, and competences for those tasks are identified. A person with certain competences should be able to successfully perform job tasks which should lead to the attainment of end results.

The interviewer starts with job tasks. Every job contains key tasks which must be performed at a high level in order for the output to meet a standard. If an applicant has held a similar job, the interviewer could query the applicant about task performance. However, many job applicants have not held the exact same job. Some may not have held jobs at the level of the open job (the new job would be a promotion). In such cases, the interviewer must infer future performance from past experience. A job task can often be translated into an employee competence.

HRM specialists have defined numerous competence factors as the result of their experience. A glossary of competence factors is contained in Appendix 3.A.

SKILL, KNOWLEDGE, AND ABILITY

A task may be defined in terms of a competence or in terms of skill, knowledge, or ability. Skill, knowledge, and ability are commonly used terms in the United States because they are specified outcomes of job analysis according to the Uniform Guidelines on Employee Selection. Skills and abilities can be inferred from job tasks in the same way that one infers competence.

Knowledge is obtained from education and work experience. During the position analysis, one must ascertain what knowledge is required to perform the job at a high level of success. For some jobs, job knowledge is easy to pin down. For example, many civil service and trade jobs have knowledge bases which can be measured by subject matter questions. For other jobs, knowledge may be more difficult to define. Many jobs require contact with people, highly technical learning experience, or knowing a field from the inside. Such knowledge must be made manifest in the employee competence identified as dealing with this aspect of the job. Knowledge is also easy to define if it results from formal education or training. Knowledge may be job specific, for example, knowledge of a procedure or knowledge of confidential information. In these cases, the competence factors must reflect the particular knowledge required. In other cases, knowledge can be defined as possession of a particular academic degree or qualification. Knowledge can also be defined in terms of reaching an acceptable score on a test.

A problem arises from the fact that job incumbents are frequently unaware of the position's required skills, knowledge, and abilities. Job incumbents may not be able to tell the interviewer this information. Another problem is that job incumbents may exaggerate job requirements. It is up to the interviewer to determine which employee skills, knowledge, and abilities are, indeed, required and which are merely a reflection of the personality or an ambition of the current job incumbent. The interviewer must make a determination which skills, knowledge, and abilities are needed in a particular job.

JOB REQUIREMENTS

Some employee competence factors are tied to the regulations governing a field of work. For example, possession of a license, completion of an apprenticeship, passing a civil service examination, or obtaining a certificate for completion of an educational program are all competence factors. The interviewer does not need to translate them.

AN EXAMPLE

In the following example, a series of sample job tasks are detailed:

1. Communicate and receive information by telephone
2. Writes reports
3. Performs routine calculations
4. Provides technical information
5. Word processes from written copy
6. Checks own work for accuracy and completeness
7. Develops agenda for meetings and conferences
8. Makes decisions and takes independent action
9. Write, modify, or debug programs in computer languages
10. Deal with angry or noncooperative people

A job task is matched with an employee competence factor. The process of matching job tasks and employee competence factors is judgmental. It is assumed that the judgment will be assisted by data made available from a job analysis. Any manager who is familiar with the competence-based method of employment interviewing should be able to exercise the necessary judgment. Oftentimes a SME, such as a supervisor, a job analyst, or a human resource development specialist, is asked to verify the process. Each of the sample job tasks can be translated into an employee competence factor as illustrated in the following:

1. *Competence factor: Oral Communication.*   The ability to speak clearly. The ability to use language in an interesting and informative manner to communicate information within an organization. (Inferred from sample job task 1.)
2. *Competence factor: Written Communication.*   Ability to get a written message across in a clear and direct manner. (Inferred from sample job task 2.)
3. *Competence factor: Calculation.*   Making basic arithmetic calculations with speed and accuracy. (Inferred from sample job task 3.)

4. *Competence factor: Technical Translation.* Ability to translate technical documents and language into understandable form for laymen. (Inferred from sample job task 4.)

5. *Competence factor: Word processing at certain level of proficiency.* Ability to process x words per minute with y level of accuracy. (Inferred from sample job task 5.)

6. *Competence factor: Attention to detail.* Ability to work accurately with large amounts of data, and to follow up to see if objectives are accomplished. (Inferred from sample job task 6.)

7. *Competence factor: Planning and organizing.* Setting goals for accomplishment of objectives. Developing a course of action and implementing the course of action in order to accomplish goals within an established time frame. Structuring activities in order to maximize effectiveness of one's time. (Inferred from sample job task 7.)

8. *Competence factor: Independent work.* Ability to work without supervision and perform to a predetermined level. (Inferred from sample job task 8.)

9. *Competence factor: Decision making.* Ability to evaluate relevant information, recognize alternatives, and reach conclusions based on the evidence. (Inferred from sample job task 8.)

10. *Competence factor: Human relations skill.* Being aware of needs of colleagues and co-workers, and taking those needs into consideration when making decisions. (Inferred from sample job task 10.)

11. *Competence factor: Stress tolerance.* The ability to work under conditions of high pressure, competition, adversity, and maintain a high level of performance. (Inferred from sample job task 10.)

12. *Competence factor: Computer logic proficiency.* Proficiency in producing code and effectiveness in identifying problems and modifying sequence of operations of computer program statement. (Inferred from sample job task 9.)

13. *Competence factor: Initiative.* Taking action to start projects, to keep projects going despite adversity, and to exert effort to meet project goals. (Inferred from sample job task 8.)

It is a challenge to develop employee competence factors from job tasks. Tasks are specific; employee competence is abstract and behavioral. One should be sure that any employee competences one develops are measurable. The interviewer will be obtaining data on these competences during the interview, and he/she will be evaluating this information against hiring criteria (standards) after the interview.

IDENTIFYING FUTURE COMPETENCES

Taylor and O'Driscoll (1995) note that in some cases competences must be identified for the future "when either the job is expected to change in some way, or those being hired for the position are also being selected for their potential to perform future jobs to which they are likely to be promoted. In both cases, subject matter experts must identify the anticipated job end results and tasks." (25)

USE OF THE RESUMÉ AND APPLICATION BLANK IN PREPARING FOR THE INTERVIEW

The interviewer seeks to develop an understanding of the applicant prior to the interview. The examination of the applicant's resumé and application form will yield information for the development of questions and a chronological record of the applicant's academic and work-related activities.

Much of the basic information about an applicant can be obtained from the documents they submit to the prospective employer. The organization will have an application form which will call for factual information about the applicant's background. The applicants will have a resumé which will present a chronological record of their educational background and work experience. The first thing to do with these documents is to analyze the applicant's record to see if it is complete.

The applicant will strive to put his/her best foot forward in the employment process. Applicants do not realize that an employer wants a complete picture of their background, so they present their strong points and tend to leave out the weak ones. The interviewer seeks to obtain a complete chronological record. This means that the interviewer will account for all the applicant's time both in school and after school. Time which cannot be accounted for is a gap, and the interviewer will want to get an explanation for any gaps. Gaps may be caused by illness, periods of unemployment, child care, personal problems, school problems, work problems, or many other reasons. While the interview should not be a search for negative information, the interview is the only opportunity the interviewer will have to develop a complete chronology. Most applications and resumés are set up in chronological order to facilitate this matter. A skilled interviewer will note the gaps in an applicant's record and plan to fill them in during the interview. The interviewer will seek to use the information obtained previous to the interview to help frame questions aimed at obtaining information relevant to one or more of the qualities sought in job applicants.

The resumé and application form is also useful to the interviewer in tailoring questions to specific applicants. In the structured interview the goal is to ask the same questions of each applicant. However, with the exception of the most highly structured interviews, it is appropriate to modify questions to accommodate what the interviewer already knows about the applicant.

DEVELOPING JOB-RELATED QUESTIONS

The final phase of preparation for the interview is the development of questions and a schedule for asking them. In the approach suggested in this book, the interviewer develops questions designed to yield information relating to employee competence factors. In order for evaluation to take place after the interview, sufficient data relative to each employee competence factor must be obtained. A way to assure that sufficient data are obtained is to plan ahead.

There is now a debate about whether the typical questions used by employment interviewers should be used at all. Lists of suggested or popular interview questions are common. The typical questions pose two problems. The first is that applicants are often well prepared for the typical questions. This may prevent the interviewer from gaining insight into the applicant's job-related behavior. The second is that interviewers may not be able to establish the job relatedness of some of the typical questions. If typical questions are used, their job relatedness should be established by job analysis or the critical incident technique. On the plus side interviewers should recognize that the employment interview is not a test. The typical questions give the interviewer and interviewee a common ground for discussion. It is up to both parties to make the interview productive. For most interviews, job experience, education, interests, and activities have direct relevance. However, it is up to the interviewer to focus in on those aspects of the applicant's experience which are most relevant to the competence factors identified for the open position.

Field and Gatewood (1989) point out that researchers criticize the traditional method of asking the same questions of applicants for different jobs. "Rather than selecting existing questions, they have recommended the use of job analysis in developing interview content. They have argued that a study should be made of the job for which the interview will be used. Questions should then be based on the important requirements of the job." (146)

For applicants who have had work experience, especially experience in jobs which are similar to the open job, there will be many opportunities to develop questions. The interviewer tries to have at least 3 to 4 questions for each competence factor on which he/she plans to rate the applicant. It is possible that some questions will not draw out material which is useful for evaluation later on. So the interviewer should be prepared to extend his/her questioning until he/she has sufficient material for subsequent rating. Once the interviewer has achieved rapport with an applicant, he/she can proceed to ask prepared questions.

The tie-in between position analysis and the subsequent steps in the interview process is crucial. The questions to be developed are based on the position to be filled. Mirabile (1994) describes this process as follows:

Once we'd agreed on the most critical success factors for the sales position, it became possible to select the top 10 factors and construct a series of open-ended questions that helped interviewers determine whether job candidates were likely to succeed in the position. For instance, if an interviewer was trying to find out if the candidate was tenacious, she could ask "What do you typically do when you meet continued resistance from a prospective customer?" Or, to probe communication skills: "Describe a situation in which you feel your communication ability really made a positive difference in the outcome." (72)

The information provided by the interviewee during the interview will be analyzed to see if the candidate has experience or potential which is consistent with the success factors identified in the position analysis.

Behavioral incidents obtained from a critical incident analysis may be used not only to develop questions but also to provide guidance in documenting interviewees' responses to questions. By discovering the range of possible interviewee responses to questions before the formal interview process begins, the interviewer is better prepared for the evaluation process. The interviewer will then know what constitutes excellence on a competence factor, what constitutes having acceptable qualifications on a competence factor, and what constitutes below-average performance. A successful interview will generate enough behavioral information to enable the interviewer to rate the applicant on relevant factors and to make appropriate documentation.

Appendix 3.B gives examples of questions and related competence dimensions. These general examples of job-related questions will be useful to interviewers as they develop questions for their specific circumstances.

BEHAVIOR DESCRIPTION QUESTIONS

Taylor and O'Driscoll (1995) provide a methodology for developing questions to be used to elicit behavior descriptions from job applicants. In the behavior description interview, applicants are asked for examples of how they have handled situations previously identified as being job related. Questions are developed to elicit information relevant to specific competences which are inferred from these situations. The goal of this form of questioning is to elicit from applicants what they have done as opposed to what they think should be done.

According to Taylor and O'Driscoll (1995), a behavior description by a job applicant should consist of three components, namely, the situation, the actual behavior of the candidate in the situation, and the outcome of the situation. Each behavioral description question entails an open-ended question to the applicant to elicit a description of the situation. These open-ended questions are developed previous to the interview. Critical incidents from the position analysis are an ideal basis of identifying situations about which to inquire. The open-ended question about a situation results not only in a description of a situation by the applicant but also informs the interviewer whether the applicant has ever been in such a situation. If the applicant explains that he/she is not familiar with such a situation, the interviewer may go on to another open-ended question. If the applicant indicates that he/she has been involved in such a situation, the interviewer could then ask the applicant to relate the most recent example (or any example—interviewees can describe any situation they choose as long as one specific situation has been chosen). Probe questions are used to elicit as much information as possible about the behavior of the applicant in the situation. Such probe questions can be developed before the interview or can be developed during the interview. After the first situation has been described, the interviewer may ask for additional examples (i.e., situations).

The interviewer must be careful not to reveal the competences of interest to the employer to the applicant. By indicating the competence of interest in the question, the interviewer has posed a leading question to the applicant. Interviewers are encouraged to ask applicants about negative situations, as well as positive situations (although most of the situations described by applicants probably will be positive).

Taylor and O'Driscoll (1995) suggest that some typical questions asked in employment interviews are not appropriate for the behavior description interview. Applicants should not be given a chance to improve upon a response to an interviewer's question if the behavior description offered by the applicant does not indicate competence. The question, If you had it to do over again, what would you do differently? is ruled out. The typical question, What are your strengths and weaknesses? is ruled out as well. The applicant's response must be considered to be subjective. It would be best for the interviewer to judge the applicant's strengths and weaknesses based on behavior descriptions offered by the applicant.

In the behavior description question format, the same question need not be asked of each applicant. Rather questions are tailored to be specific to each applicant. This is the case for the first question as well as for follow-up questions. The applicant's resumé or application form is often the basis for the interviewer to tailor questions. Consistency is achieved by making sure each applicant is asked questions regarding each competence considered important for the open position. This is referred to as a patterned interview, according to Taylor and O'Driscoll (1995). This means that the interviewer follows a pattern of questions rather than asking each applicant identical questions.

Behavior description questions are ideal for applicants who have had little work experience (e.g., recent graduates). Such applicants can be asked about relevant behavior in educational settings or in nonwork settings.

Taylor and O'Driscoll (1995) advise that all questions be reviewed by someone familiar with behavior description interviewing prior to their use. The review should be conducted by someone independent of the question development process in order to assure objectivity.

QUESTIONS ABOUT INTENTIONS

Question development has been aimed at eliciting information from applicants about their past experience. However, there will be occasions when the interviewer will wish to pose hypothetical questions. These occasions are a new job, jobs for which the competences have changed considerably, and jobs for which a critical incident analysis are impractical. The best examples of this approach are the situational interview method of Latham (1989) and the highly structured interview approach of Campion, Pursell, and Brown (1988).

Questions about behavioral intentions allow the interviewer to expand the range of the interview beyond background information. Another advantage of the behavioral intention questions is that they may be asked of each applicant in a standardized manner (a situational test question). Such standardization is consistent with a nondiscriminatory approach to employment interviewing.

Taylor and O'Driscoll (1995) suggest a methodology for the development of behavior intention questions. They assume that a critical incident analysis will be conducted prior to the question development process. The interviewer develops two or three questions for each job-related competence. Question development proceeds from a critical incident which is turned into a question. This can be done by preceding the critical incident with the question, What would you do in this situation? An essential step in the development of behavior intention questions is the development of a scoring procedure for applicant responses. The rating form proposed in Chapter 5 must be modified to be used with behavior intention questions. Instead of being rated, the applicant's responses are scored.

Taylor and O'Driscoll (1995) recommend the following procedure for developing a scoring key for interview questions. To begin, a list of possible applicant responses is developed. This may be done by SMEs or job incumbents. The possible answers to each question are placed on a scale. A three- or five-point scale may be used. Scaling is done by means of a panel of SMEs, which takes the pool of possible responses and makes judgments about which responses are unacceptable (incompetent), acceptable, and very good (highly competent). An acceptable or very good response is judged to lead to favorable outcomes on the job. Once these scales have been developed they will become the basis for evaluating a candidate's suitability for the job.

According to Taylor and O'Driscoll (1995), behavior intention questions and scoring keys should have the following characteristics: The full range of possible candidates' responses should be included in the scoring key; questions which do not differentiate between candidates should be eliminated; and, ideally, the predictive validity of each question should be established.

An example will clarify how a behavioral intention question is developed. The following example based on the position of Public Assistance Clerk is given by Field and Gatewood (1989, 155–156):

1. *The relevant job task.*   Meets with and assists agency clients through personal contacts in the completion of agency forms, determination of public assistance checks, and interpretation of agency eligibility requirements in order to facilitate distribution of public assistance funds from the state.

2. *Skill, knowledge, or ability (competence factor).*   Ability to interact tactfully with agency clients on a face-to-face basis.

3. *Interview question.*   A client of your state agency walks up to your desk. She says she was told that a check she was due from the agency was sent five days ago. She

claims she has not received the check. She says she has bills to pay, and no one will help her. She is very angry. How would you handle this situation?

4. *Rating scale.* Low rating: Tell her you will try to find the person with whom she talked, and you will have that person call her. Average rating: Apologize and tell her you will have to check into the problem and call her in a day or two. High rating: Try to calm her and investigate the problem while she waits.

OTHER TYPES OF STRUCTURED INTERVIEW QUESTIONS

In the structured interview approach, the interviewer is constrained as compared to the traditional approach or an in-depth (clinical) approach. The interviewer develops a schedule of questions and applies this schedule to all applicants. It is important to develop the best possible questions. The following suggestions have been made by researchers to aid the practitioner in perfecting his/her question development technique. Campion, Pursell, and Brown (1991) describe three types of questions, namely the job knowledge question, the job sample (or simulation) question, and worker requirements questions. Job knowledge questions deal with technical aspects of the job. They could also deal with basic knowledge which is essential to learn the job. Questions could assess basic educational skills, such as reading, writing, and mathematics. An interview comprised of many of these questions would resemble an oral test. Job knowledge and requirements questions could also cover very complex technical or management skills.

An ideal form of interview is composed of job sample questions. Most of us are familiar with the ultimate job sample interview, the road test, administered by motor vehicle department personnel. In some cases job applicants are asked to perform actual job tasks during an interview. A famous example from history is the eye–hand coordination test used by the U.S. Army Air Force to select pilots in World War II. The word processing test is another form of job sample test. Simulations are common in group assessment procedures, such as assessment centers. They can also be developed for individual administration in an interview. For example, a job applicant could be asked to participate in a role play with the interviewer. Simulation questions could take the form of a hypothetical issue. Job applicants could be asked to respond to hypothetical questions. Their responses would be evaluated in terms of their correct use of terminology or the accuracy of the examples they provide.

Worker requirements questions are related to job requirements (employee specifications in job description terminology). Educational background is a common worker requirement. This issue is also one of the most typical sources of interview questions. Frequently there are requirements about job related travel, shift work, and relocation. These issues could also generate worker requirements questions.

Bell (1992) proposes the following seven types of interview questions for use in structured interviews: definitional questions, causal questions, hypothetical questions, situational questions, simulation questions, relational questions, and explanatory questions. The definitional question usually posed is, What is a _____? or, What does _____ refer to or mean? They require applicants to demonstrate their knowledge of terms, concepts, and tools used at work. The causal question posed is What happens when_____? or, What is the result of_____? According to Bell, hypothetical questions test the applicant's ability to handle future situations based on past learning and experience. These questions are, What would you do if_____? or, What could happen if_____? This form of question is similar to the situational interview format proposed by Campion, Pursell, and Brown (1981) and Latham (1989). According to Bell, the relational question asks the applicant to tell, perhaps by role playing, how he or she would handle interpersonal situations. In order to assess job knowledge, Bell proposes explanatory questions such as, Why would you_____? or, Why do you_____? or, How would you explain_____?

Taylor and O'Driscoll (1995) propose the following three types of questions to assess an applicant's technical knowledge: (1) an applicant can be asked to provide behavior descriptions of situations where he/she used a technology; (2) applicants can be asked a behavior intention question which focuses on a technical issue; and (3) questions can be developed to test technical knowledge (job knowledge questions). Taylor and O'Driscoll identify another form of structured interview question—the willingness question. Frequently encountered issues in employment interviewing involve willingness to do shift work, to travel extensively for business, to relocate, and to tolerate certain physical working conditions. These issues do not lend themselves to open-ended questions. The interviewer poses yes–no questions to the applicant in order to ascertain the applicant's willingness to accept the particular working condition.

QUESTION BANK

Nevo and Berman (1994) caution employers that applicants can learn about structured interview procedures through word of mouth. If this occurs the interview validity will be compromised. An important recommendation is made to avoid this problem. Employers who interview frequently and regularly for the same position openings are advised to develop alternative questions for each employee competence. By substituting equivalent questions on a random basis, the ability of applicants to rehearse will be minimized.

A CASE STUDY

In order to illustrate concepts, a hypothetical case is presented. One can assume that the open job is that of an assistant manager in a retail clothing store. The store sells a full line of women's clothing. It consists of 2,000 square feet of selling space, and it has a total staff of eleven, including, the manager, an assistant manager, a stock person, and eight sales associates or floor people. While stores vary in many ways, the job of the assistant manager is fairly standard. The key tasks performed by the assistant store manager are as follows:

1. Conducts sales transactions with customers
2. Handles cash and operates electronic cash register
3. Completes documents on merchandise returns, layaways, and exchanges
4. Responsible for opening and closing the store
5. Supervises sales personnel
6. Designs merchandising displays in store and in store windows
7. Maintains store security and follows required security procedures
8. Knows current fashion trends and the store's merchandise lines
9. Solves problems related to store operation, HRM, and customer service
10. Performs other duties as requested by the store manager

These tasks would be filled in on the Competence Model Worksheet. A sample worksheet for the assistant store manager is provided in Figure 3.2 as an example. A blank Competence Model Worksheet is included in this chapter as Appendix 3.C.

APPENDIX 3.A
GLOSSARY OF COMPETENCE FACTORS

The factors defined represent only a sample of the many job-related behavioral factors which can be sought after in job candidates. They should be regarded as a starting point. The interviewer may develop additional competence factors which are specifically related to an open position.

achievement motivation A desire to excel or succeed in competitive situations as evidenced by taking responsibility and taking calculated risks to achieve goals.

adaptability The ability to make changes in one's self or one's behavior in order to deal with changing circumstances, changing living conditions, and changing levels in organizational hierarchy.

analysis The ability to assimilate information from various sources and develop findings based on the analysis of that information.

attention to detail Perception of key aspects of a situation. Taking details into consideration during the planning process.

calculating skill Making basic arithmetic calculations with speed and accuracy.

career interest A knowledge of realistic career prospects for an individual, including salary aspirations and knowledge of job duties of advanced positions.

control Establishes goals for subordinates or for one's area of responsibility. Checks to assure conformity with the plan and follows up on deviations from the plan.

Figure 3.2
Competence Model Worksheet for Assistant Manager Position

Instructions for Competence Modeling

In order to fill in the blanks in **Step 1**, one may use the critical incident technique or the job analysis technique.

In **Step 2**, competence factors are identified. Competence factors are descriptions of behaviors which lead to successful job performance. Refer to the glossary of competence factors to select those factors which are appropriate to work activities of the open position.

Step 3 requires the development of questions which will elicit behavior descriptions relating to the competence factors. Behavior description questions elicit information about educational background, work experience, and interests and activities. Other types of questions which could be developed are job knowledge questions, behavioral intention questions, or worker require— ments questions. Probe questions are developed to elicit further information from the applicant.

Step 1: **Position Analysis**   Job Title _Assistant Manager_

Task Description or Critical Incident	Competence Code	Success Factor Code
Conducts sales transaction with customers	S	3
Handles cash and operates electronic cash register	S	2
Completes documents on merchandise returns, layaways, and exchanges	S	2
Responsible for opening and closing the store	S	3
Supervises sales personnel	S	3
Designs merchandising displays in store and in store windows	S	2
Maintains store security and follows required security procedures	S	3
Knows current fashion trends and the store's merchandise lines	K	2
Performs other duties as requested by the store manager	S	1

Competence Code	
Skill	S
Knowledge	K
Ability	A

Success Factor Code	
Extremely Important to Job Success	3
Moderately Important to Job Success	2
Slightly Important to Job Success	1

Figure 3.2 *(continued)*

Step 2: **Identification of Competence Factors**

Competence Code	Success Factor Code	Competence Factor
S	3	Previous experience in retailing
S	3	Interpersonal skill
K	2	Educational background
A	1	Career interest

Competence Code	
Skill	S
Knowledge	K
Ability	A

Success Factor Code	
Extremely Important to Job Success	3
Moderately Important to Job Success	2
Slightly Important to Job Success	1

Figure 3.2 *(continued)*

Step 3:   **Question Development**

Competence Factor: _____ Educational Background _____

Comprehensive Question:

What courses have you taken that relate to the open Assistant Store Manager

position?

Probe: _____ High School and College G.P.A. _____

Competence Factor: _____ Career Interest _____

Comprehensive Question:

Explain to me your knowledge of fashion trends.

Could you tell me about some of the perceptions of the current fashion?

Tell me about the vision you have for your career in retailing.

Probe: _____

Competence Factor: _____ Work Experience _____

Comprehensive Question:

How have you handled shoplifting in the past?   Probe: As needed

I see in your previous job you did layaways. Please explain the procedures you

used.   Probe: as needed.

Tell me about your sales experience in your previous retail jobs.

Tell me how you would conduct a sales transaction. Be sure to include all the

details of the transaction that you can anticipate.

In your previous retail experience you worked with cash. Please describe your

experience.

(ALTERNATE QUESTION): I see that you have been in retail sales previously. Can

you tell me how you conducted a sales transaction on that job? Please detail for

me the specific steps you would follow in assisting a customer.

Probe: _____ Did you have a sales quota? _____

40

Figure 3.2 *(continued)*

Competence Factor: Work Experience (continued)

Comprehensive Question:

Imagine an empty store window in our shop. Tell me what kind of a display you

would put in it and how you would design and implement the display. Be as specific

as possible.

Probe:

Competence Factor: Interpersonal Skill

Comprehensive Question:

How would you interact with customers, associates, and managers in your Assistant

Manger role?

Probe:

Competence Factor:

Comprehensive Question:

Probe:

counseling Acts in a coaching role to help subordinates overcome problems. Makes suggestions for performance improvement and follows up to see if performance improvement is accomplished.

creativity Developing imaginative solutions to problems, the generation of new ideas, the translation of an innovative idea into a new product, service, or method of production.

decisiveness The willingness to make quick or timely decisions in order to accomplish results.

delegation of authority Willingness and ability to authorize subordinates to take action to reach goals of the supervisor. Giving the subordinate a broad outline of what needs to be done and when it needs to be done and leaving the rest to the subordinate.

dominance A tendency to influence events in an aggressive manner in group or organizational settings.

educational background The relevance of a person's education to the knowledge required by the job.

educational quality A person's educational achievements as measured by grade point average, the accreditation of the school, and the overall standing of the school.

energy Works with enthusiasm and dynamism in group or organizational settings.

efficiency Having and using the requisite skills, knowledge, and ability. Concern for effective performance.

financial analysis Reads and interprets financial tables and uses financial data to develop an understanding of the organization.

first impact The ability to manage one's impression on others, especially at outset of relationships.

human relations sensitivity Being aware of needs of colleagues and co-workers and taking those needs into consideration when making decisions.

independence Taking a stand even though it may be unpopular. Speaking with candor under all conditions.

initiative Taking action to start projects, to keep projects going despite adversity, and to exert effort to meet project goals.

interests and activities The participation in significant activities outside one's line of work. The taking on of a significant role in such an activity.

interpersonal skills Managing interactions in a work setting in a pleasant and effective manner. The ability to relate to coworkers at various levels, including higher and lower levels.

judgment Develops a set of alternatives, evaluates alternatives, and reaches a sound decision. Chooses the best alternative. Reaching decisions which take into consideration the organization's needs, the choice of the best alternative, and the likelihood of the success of the outcome of the decision.

keypunching Data entry into computer terminal. Performance includes speed and accuracy.

leadership Able to develop a sense of the mission of the organization or group and take action to influence others to work towards accomplishment of the mission.

listening Making the necessary effort to understand another person's point. Avoiding distractions in two-way communication. Being empathetic with someone who is communicating to us.

management skills Strategic planning, directing, controlling and monitoring work, training, information gathering, advising and counseling subordinates, policy making, disciplining and terminating, allocating resources, and coordination (not all skills may be relevant for a given position).

mathematical ability Able to solve arithmetic problems.

maturity Showing control in the face of stress or adverse circumstances in organizational settings. Having an understanding of an impact of one's behavior in organizational settings.

mental ability Intelligence level of an individual as measured by verbal ability, mathematical ability, the capacity to reason logically, and the ability to learn in organizational settings.

motivating others Managing others based on a motivational premise, such as, rewards, enthusiasm, role modeling, or meeting others' needs through work.

negotiating skill Entering into give-and-take discussions with others so as to produce outcomes acceptable to both parties.

oral communication The ability to speak clearly. The ability to use language in an interesting and informative manner to communicate information within an organization. The ability to lead meetings or participate in meetings. Making effective formal presentations when given time to prepare.

organizational loyalty Desire to remain with organization despite ups and downs of day-to-day problems, and a likelihood of maintaining a long tenure in an organization.

organization sensitivity Understands impact of an action on other units of the organization.

patience Allowing subordinates sufficient time to complete their objectives before intervening. Avoiding a rush to judgment in decision making.

persuasiveness Ability to forcefully present one's point of view in such a manner that it will influence others. The ability to make convincing presentations in order to elicit participation in one's goals.

persistence Special effort in a course of action in order to reach goals. Activity maintained in spite of difficulties. Unremitting perseverance.

planning and organizing Setting goals for accomplishment of objectives. Developing a course of action and implementing the course of action in order to accomplish goals within an established time frame. Structuring activities in order to maximize effectiveness of one's time.

problem analysis Identifies cause of problems through investigation of the symptoms the problem manifests in the organization.

reading ability The ability to read and understand written material.

recency of education The extent to which a person's educational background corresponds with current knowledge requirements of the job, and the extent to which an individual has maintained currency in their education.

results orientation A focus on delivering promised results. Not accepting excuses for missed deadlines or unacceptable work.

risk profile A person's preference for risk. A person may be a high risk taker at one extreme or averse to risk at another. Moderate risk taking is associated with achievement orientation.

sensitivity Showing awareness of and concern for others' feelings in work-related situations. Showing compassion for a coworker's or subordinate's misfortunes.

stress tolerance The ability to work under conditions of high pressure, competition, adversity, and maintain a high level of performance.

supervisory relations Developing trust with the supervisor. Having open communications with the supervisor. Acceptance of the supervisor's management style.

team building Focusing on group rather than individual goals. Building team spirit in a group. Fostering intergroup cooperation.

technical ability Able to utilize the core technologies of a job in order to produce expected results

technical translation Works with technical material or technical discipline and translates that material into a form which will be understandable and useful for laymen.

turnover risk Previous behavior indicates that the applicant may not remain employed long enough to make a meaningful contribution to the employer.

typing Operates manual, electric, or word processing machine. Includes typing from dictation.

work attitude Extent to which an individual maintains a positive attitude towards the job, superiors, and coworkers.

work experience The relevance of previous work experience to the current job opening as measured by similarity in terms of tasks performed, complexity of the tasks, and organizational context (situation).

written communication skills The ability to write clearly. The ability to draft documents and other communications. The ability to present one's thoughts in an effective manner in writing.

Similar versions of competence factors are used by many HRM practitioners and consultants. References for published versions of these concepts are Taylor and O'Driscoll (1995), Gatewood and Field (1990), Janz, Hellervik, and Gilmore (1986), Thornton and Byham (1982, 138–140), and Moffat (1979).

APPENDIX 3.B
SAMPLE QUESTIONS

The process of developing questions is based on the employee competences sought in applicants. In this appendix, the reader can examine a broader list of sample questions which tie together tasks and employee competence. These questions can be asked of any applicant. If the question does not yield information related to the employee competence factor, it can be repeated or a probe can be used. The interviewer can modify these questions as needed. For example, if behavior descriptions are sought from applicants, they may be asked to identify a specific situation before these questions are asked. Applicants are then asked to describe their behavior in the situation and the outcome.

Competence Factor: Achievement Motivation

- Name two of your best accomplishments, including where the assignments came from, your plans in carrying them out, how you eventually did carry them out, and any obstacles you overcame.
- What do you consider your greatest accomplishments in your present position?
- Describe your accomplishments in community-related activities.

  Probes:
  - What sparked your interest in this activity?
  - What did you gain from this activity?

- What would be your greatest success to date?
- What was the most difficult task or assignment you confronted in these jobs, and how did you deal with it?

Competence Factor: Attention to Detail

- Describe a course, project, or work experience which was complex.

  Probes:
  - What kind of follow-up did you undertake?
  - How much time was spent on unexpected difficulties?

Competence Factor: Career Interest

- What led to your choice of the career you are planning?
- Why did or did you not attend college (or graduate school, trade school, and so forth)?
- Why did you choose to major in this particular field?
- How did you select your college or university?
- Have you devised a career plan? If so, what is it, and how did you arrive at it?
- Do you have long- and short-range work goals or objectives? When and why did you establish them, and how are you going to attain them?
- How does this job work into your overall career plan?
- What factors have been most important in your development to date?
- Have you done anything to improve yourself in recent years?

- What accomplishments would you like to make in the next five years?
- Where do you see yourself five years from now, with regard to a career?
- What is your vision of yourself ten years from now?
- Have there been any obstacles hindering your ability to move ahead faster? If so, what?

Competence Factor: Creativity

- Can you think of a situation where innovation was required at work?

Probe:
  - What did you do in this situation?

Competence Factor: Decision Making

- Discuss an important decision you have made regarding work or school.

Probe:
  - What factors influenced your decision?

Competence Factor: Educational Background

- What college subjects did you like best? Why?
- What college subjects did you like least? Why?
- What aspects of your education or training have prepared you for this job?
- How has your college experience prepared you for your working career?

Competence Factor: Human Relations Skill

- Tell me about a course, work experience, or extracurricular activity where you had to work closely with others.

Probes:
  - How did it go?
  - How did you overcome any difficulties?

- Tell me about a work experience where you had to work with the public.

Probe:
  - How did you handle irate customers?

- When was the last time you worked with someone to accomplish a task? Can you tell me about it?

Probes:
  - How were the tasks divided between both of you?
  - Did you encounter any obstacles along the way? If so, how did you handle them?

- Who did you find the most difficult person you had to deal with? Describe an interaction which illustrates that difficulty.

  Probes:
  - Tell me about the last time you dealt with him/her?
  - What was the situation?
  - What did the two of you have to say?
  - How did you resolve the situation?
  - How do you manage subordinates who report to you?

Competence Factor: Independent Work/Initiative

- Have you taken an independent study course? Describe it.
- Describe some work responsibilities which you had to accomplish on your own.
- Describe a project you started on your own.

  Probes:
  - What did you do?
  - Why did you do it?

- Can you think of a company policy that needed changing? What did you do in order to effect the change?
- What have you done on your present job that goes beyond what was required?

Competence Factor: Leadership

- Discuss a work situation in which you felt you successfully directed the work of others or marshalled resources.
- Give an example of your ability to manage or supervise others.
- What are the most important performance expectations in your area? How have you monitored the work in this area?

Competence Factor: Learning Ability

- Tell me about a job you had which required you to learn new things.
- Tell me about a recent job or experience which you would describe as a real learning experience.

  Probe:
  - What did you learn from the job or the experience?

- Discuss the highlights of your most recent educational experience.

  Probes:
  - What led you to the choice of your major?
  - Best subjects? Subjects done less well?

- Subjects liked most? Liked least?
- Do you feel your grades reflected your efforts?
- Any special achievements?
- Most difficult problems?

Competence Factor: Motivation

- Can you tell me why you are interested in this particular job?
- What are your long- and short-range goals at this point?
- Are you satisfied with this line of work?
- What are the pros and cons of this line of work in your opinion?
- Name a few things most important to you in your job.
- If you had to pick a favorite job, which one you would you choose?

Competence Factor: Organization Commitment

- Can you think of some examples where you did work above and beyond the norm?

  Probes:
  - What did you do?
  - Why were you chosen for it?
  - How did you feel about this?

Competence Factor: Planning and Organizing

- Describe a project you had to control.

  Probe:
  - What did you do?

- Of all the assignments which you have been given, which do you consider to have required the greatest amount of effort? How did you go about accomplishing this assignment?

  Probes:
  - Discuss the assignment.
  - Tell me how you handled it.
  - Was the assignment completed on time?

- Can you describe something you have implemented at work?

  Probe:
  - Ask about planning issues.

Competence Factor: Problem Analysis

- When you have been made aware of, or have discovered yourself, a problem in your work performance, what was your course of action?

Probe:
- Can you give me an example?

- In some aspects of work it is important to be free of error. Can you describe a situation where you have tried to prevent errors?

Probes:
- What did you do?
- Outcome?

- Can you think of a situation where you had to solve a problem at work? What did you do in this situation?

Competence Factor: Stress Tolerance

- Describe a situation where you had to work under pressure.

Probes:
- What kind of pressure?
- How did you cope?

- When was the last time you felt pressure on a job?

Probes:
- How did the situation come about?
- How did you react?
- What made you decide to handle it that way?
- What effect, if any, did this have on your other responsibilities?

- Discuss the last time you made a decision when your instructions about what to do were ambiguous or contradictory.

Probes:
- What was the source of confusion?
- Did you seek clarification or counsel?
- What were the reactions of others to your decision?

Competence Factor: Technical Ability

- Tell me about your work in mathematics.

Probes:

- What grades did you receive?
- What was most difficult? Easy?

- I noticed on your resumé that you attended _____ training program. Can you describe the training program?

Probe:

- How did you do?
- How have you made use of the course at work?

Competence Factor: Turnover Risk

- Did you help finance your own education? How and why?
- Do you plan to continue your education? Why or why not?
- Why are you leaving your present job (why did you leave your last job)?
- Do you have plans for continued study? An advanced degree?

Competence Factor: Written Communications

- Tell me about your experience in preparing written materials.

APPENDIX 3.C
COMPETENCE MODEL WORKSHEET

Instructions for Competence Modeling

In order to fill in the blanks in **Step 1**, one may use the critical incident technique or the job analysis technique.

In **Step 2**, competence factors are identified. Competence factors are descriptions of behaviors which lead to successful job performance. Refer to the glossary of competence factors in Appendix 3.A to select those factors which are appropriate to work activities of the open position.

Step 3 requires the development of questions which will elicit behavior descriptions relating to the competence factors. Behavior description questions elicit information about educational background, work experience, and interests and activities. Other types of questions which could be developed are job knowledge questions, behavioral intention questions, or worker require– ments questions. Probe questions are developed to elicit further information from the applicant.

Step 1:   **Position Analysis**   Job Title _____

Task Description or Critical Incident	Competence Code	Success Factor Code

Competence Code	
Skill	S
Knowledge	K
Ability	A

Success Factor Code	
Extremely Important to Job Success	3
Moderately Important to Job Success	2
Slightly Important to Job Success	1

Appendix 3.C *(continued)*

Step 2: Identification of Competence Factors

Competence Code	Success Factor Code	Competence Factor

Competence Code	
Skill	S
Knowledge	K
Ability	A

Success Factor Code	
Extremely Important to Job Success	3
Moderately Important to Job Success	2
Slightly Important to Job Success	1

Appendix 3.C *(continued)*

Step 3:   Question Development

Competence Factor: _____
Comprehensive Question:

_____

_____

_____

_____

Probe: _____

Competence Factor: _____
Comprehensive Question:

_____

_____

_____

_____

Probe: _____

Competence Factor: _____
Comprehensive Question:

_____

_____

_____

_____

Probe: _____

Competence Factor: _____
Comprehensive Question:

_____

_____

_____

_____

Probe: _____

Appendix 3.C *(continued)*

Competence Factor: _____

Comprehensive Question:

_____

_____

_____

_____

Probe: _____

Competence Factor: _____

Comprehensive Question:

_____

_____

_____

_____

Probe: _____

Competence Factor: _____

Comprehensive Question:

_____

_____

_____

_____

Probe: _____

Competence Factor: _____

Comprehensive Question:

_____

_____

_____

_____

Probe: _____

Chapter Four

Interviewing Techniques

Once preparation has been completed, the interviewer is ready to conduct an employment interview. There are additional complexities in employment interviewing which are not covered by preparation. However, most of the additional complexity in employment interviewing involves the interviewer's style. Style is an intangible in the conduct of the interview. The interview should resemble a conversation! It should place the interviewee at ease while covering personal information. It should be stimulating and the organization should come through as a good place to work. Fortunately, all interviewers can develop a distinctive and effective style through practice. One will find that with practice and experience that one's ability to conduct interviews will improve to the point that the process is enjoyable, purposeful, and of benefit to the organization.

The model of the competence-based interviewing process, illustrated in Figure 4.1, reveals that the interview itself is relatively straightforward. If the interviewer has done the proper preparation, the questions are developed and the rating procedures are clear. The interviewer can thus concentrate on developing rapport, obtaining answers to structured questions, using good interview techniques, taking notes, and presenting the desired image of the organization.

A major goal of the interview is to obtain information about the applicant. The kind of information one needs is outlined in Chapter 3. According to the competence-based structured interview model, the information one obtains during the interview will be used subsequently to evaluate the applicant. Another goal of the interview is to develop a good image for the organization among applicants for employment. If the interviewer works for a large organization, applicants may know something about the organization from published financial reports, magazine articles, and newspaper articles. If the organization is

Figure 4.1
Competence-Based Structured Interviewing Process—Interviewing Techniques

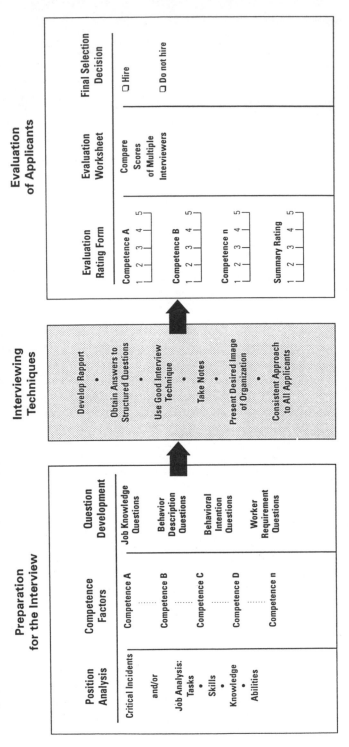

small or closely held, applicants will know little of it. Even many medium and large organizations are not well known among the public. The interviewer's contact with applicants is, therefore, the sole source of information to many people. Skillful conduct of the interview will permit one to convey the image the organization wishes to portray.

A goal for some interviewers is to portray a realistic picture of the open job. The interviewer will be able to do that toward the end of the interview; that is also the time to inform the applicant about the job in more detail. Some organizations have a procedure for giving realistic previews. It may be a booklet the interviewer hands to the applicant or even a video shown to the applicant. It has been proven that by giving such a realistic preview, an organization can reduce turnover later. Such previews will not reduce acceptance rates by applicants if the previews are handled skillfully.

Another goal of the interview is to create a desire on the part of strong applicants to join the organization and take the job. Toward the end of the employment interview, the interviewer has a chance to sell the company. In some highly structured interview procedures, the applicant does not ask questions and receive information about the job and the company at the employment interview. This is handled by a HRM professional at a separate meeting.

A final goal of the interview is the establishment of a documented record. The hire–not hire decision should be based on job-related criteria. The information obtained should be of the same kind collected for all applicants. The basis for the decision should be justifiable (objective) and fair. The Competence Model Worksheet and the Evaluation Rating Form will provide documentation of the interview.

TRADITIONAL VERSUS STRUCTURED INTERVIEW

Throughout this book the traditional interview is contrasted with the structured interview. Therefore, it will be helpful if the reader has a clear idea of what is meant by both terms. In Chapter 3, the subject of preparation for the interview is discussed. In the traditional interview, preparation consists of reviewing an applicant's application form and resumé. A job description may also be reviewed if it is available. However, job descriptions are most often developed for some other purpose than interview preparation and would therefore be only marginally useful to an interviewer. For example, two common uses of job descriptions are for compensation or for employment test validation. As is seen in Chapter 3, either job analysis or critical incident analysis is preferred in preparing for the structured interview.

Another topic taken up in Chapter 3 is defining specific competence factors to be covered in the interview. In the traditional interview, this issue is not addressed at all. It is assumed that applicants will be compared to company standards with regard to educational background and work experience. In the structured interview, specific issues to be covered in the interview are based on competence factors. Competence factors required for a specific position opening are identified as the result of job analysis or critical incident analysis.

In the traditional interview, the questions presented to the applicant are used to elicit information about the applicant's educational background, work experience, interests and activities, and work motivation. Probe questions are used to draw out the applicant and to uncover as much as possible about the applicant's background and intentions. In the structured interview, for every competence factor there is a pool of predetermined questions that is prepared. Questions during the interview are drawn from this pool. The content of the interview will not become widely known among applicants, avoiding a major pitfall of the traditional interview. In the most highly structured interviews, probe questions are not used; a question may be repeated if need be. However, in other structured interview approaches probe questions are used to follow up on structured questions to elicit further information.

In the traditional interview, the rating of the interviewee is based largely on the interviewer's intuition. In many cases there is no rating system at all. In the structured interview approach, rating scales are developed prior to the interview. The scales are based on competence factors identified in the preparation process. When making ratings the interviewer compares the applicant to a standard. The standard may be one of excellence or it may be a decision about whether or not the applicant has required qualifications.

Throughout this book the traditional and the structured interviews are contrasted. There are varying degrees of structure which may occur, and it is up to each interviewer to decide how much structure is appropriate and possible.

THE INTERVIEW SCHEDULE

Interviewers are said to follow a schedule. Since the interview is an in-depth conversation between two strangers, the schedule allows it to be comfortable and conversational despite the inevitable tension. The traditional interview schedule is chronological. There is an opening where the two strangers get acquainted. There is a series of questions covering educational background, work experience, and motivation, and there is the close where the interviewer tactfully ends the interview.

In the structured interview, the schedule is based on the questions developed to yield information on employee competence. A chronological order may not be possible. In this case the interview is referred to as a patterned interview. The interviewer will see to it that each applicant receives the same questions. The interviewer will assure that the conditions for administration of the interview remain consistent between applicants.

The interviewer has a lot of latitude as to how much of the interview schedule is written down. New interviewers tend to have all the questions written down. The competence model worksheet serves this purpose. A problem with having things written down is that referring to notes tends to make the interview too rigid and interferes with rapport. Experienced interviewers tend to memorize the interview schedule beforehand in order to improve rapport with the applicant.

GREETING THE APPLICANT

Up until now, the approach to interviewing has been very objective and rational. This is a highlight of the technique being used. However, there is an interpersonal side as well. Unless the interviewer is attuned to the emotional impact he/she is making on the applicant, many facets of the applicant will not be observed. Also, the applicant will be trying to make an emotional impact on the interviewer. The interviewer can deal with this by recording that behavior and using it later when making evaluations. The interviewer should be aware of the emotional side of the interview but should not be swayed by emotion during the interview.

Greet the applicant in a friendly manner—smile and be yourself. The interviewer introduces him/herself and gives his/her title and organizational department name. During the introduction, the interviewer notes the applicant's attire. Later, the interviewer will want to use this information to evaluate the applicant's preparation for the interview, readiness for employment, and knowledge of appropriate attire in the work environment. Sometimes, attire and appearance are job requirements. If so, there will be rating scales for these. If not, one does not let appearance assume too much importance. Many people will alter their appearance appropriately as they are socialized into the organization.

The interviewer comes out of the office to greet the applicant. This will show interest in the applicant. It will give a chance to show enthusiasm at meeting the applicant. It is a courtesy, because the applicant is unfamiliar with the layout of the office. After coming out to meet the applicant, the interviewer can then guide the applicant to a seat in the office or in an interviewing room.

Small talk seems to be the most typical topic of conversation when the interviewer first meets an applicant. If the interviewer is an outgoing person, small talk will seem perfectly natural and easy. If the interviewer is busy, small talk may seem awkward and a waste of time. Maybe a substitute can be found for small talk, but for most interviewers, small talk is the preferred approach. Small talk includes many topics, such as, the weather, how the applicant found the interviewing location, a noteworthy current event, or a mutual acquaintance. The interviewer may generate small talk about an aspect of the applicant's background gleaned from the application. Such areas as sports, hobbies, or interests would make good topics for small talk. Small talk does not have to be prolonged. It can last until the interviewer and the applicant enter the office where the interview will take place and the applicant is comfortably seated in a chair. There is no need for extended small talk, and too much small talk is bad interviewing form. It is time wasted and conveys an impression that the interview is not serious.

The key issue at the outset of the interview is the establishment of rapport. Rapport refers to a sense of mutuality between interviewer and interviewee. The area of mutual interest is in conducting the interview in a satisfactory manner. Both parties must cooperate for this to happen. Rapport is a feeling or an emotion. It does not happen by accident or as a by-product of the structured interview which will ensue. It must be created. The interviewer has the major responsibility for the development of rapport. Some things which contribute to the development of rapport with an applicant are a firm handshake, looking the interviewee in the eye, a sincere interest in the applicant, openness and candor, listening carefully to the applicant, and showing empathy. As mentioned the applicant must also contribute to the development of rapport. If he/she does not, the interviewer may use that behavior as evidence about the applicant's level of interpersonal skill. If one develops rapport with an applicant, one will find that the interview will flow easily. Applicants will trust the interviewer enough to speak openly about personal matters. The needed information will be forthcoming in a conversational manner. The interviewer will be able to devote energy to taking notes, making sure all bases are touched, and conducting an in-depth interview. The interviewer asks a minimum of questions. The interviewee takes the ball and runs with it. In the process, all major questions will be asked. The coverage will be complete because the interviewer has the chance to supplement the applicant's comments with probe questions, requests for clarification, and directions to keep the interview on track. If rapport is not achieved, the interview will be uncomfortable for both participants, and the goal of projecting a positive image for the organization will not be achieved.

Rapport may be generated rather quickly. Since the interviewer represents an organization of some standing, the applicant will want to place confidence in the meeting. One shows worthiness of such confidence by being open and frank. Rapport must be maintained throughout the interview. Many things can intervene to disturb rapport. The responsibility of the interviewer is to try to prevent such occurrences and to maintain rapport should they occur. An important thing to remember is that the applicant will be nervous about the interview. By establishing and maintaining rapport, the interviewer is taking a major step to reduce nervous feelings on the part of the applicant.

When the interview begins in earnest, the interviewer briefs the applicant on the interview to follow. The briefing will consist of a short description of the open job. At this point, the interviewer will not describe the job in detail because the goal of the interview is to have the interviewee speak about prior experience. Telling the applicant too much at the outset will lead the applicant into describing strengths and cause the applicant to avoid describing weaknesses. The applicant will be told the topics to be covered during the interview and will generally be requested to hold questions till the end. This opening segment can be rehearsed by the interviewer in advance. It is delivered in a conversational style.

THE STRUCTURED INTERVIEW

Upon completion of the preparation process, the interviewer has a very tightly scheduled interview plan. The interviewer has questions to ask and each question targets a particular competence factor (or more than one). The interviewee, however, expects to tell the interviewer information in the manner that he/she has prepared it. Most often, the interviewee plans to tell this information in chronological order. By asking the applicant to define a specific situation, to describe his/her behavior in the situation, and to define the outcome, the interviewer gives the interviewee a track to run on. Hopefully, it will be a track the applicant is able to run on. That is where the term patterned interview comes in. Since the interviewer is prepared, he/she can be flexible. The interviewer has the latitude to repeat questions if need be and to probe into areas of greatest relevance or where information is missing. Another area for flexibility concerns unexpected topics of discussion. If an applicant initiates topics which the interviewer had not anticipated in a planned question, and these topics will provide data which are related to competence factors, then the interviewer lets the applicant continue and gives encouragement to continue. At an appropriate time, the interviewer will be able to remind the applicant of the intended schedule and the interview can get back on track.

OPENING THE INTERVIEW

Once small talk has ceased and rapport has been established, the interviewer is ready to begin the interview. Some interviewers start by telling the interviewee the expected schedule. Another approach is to shift into a questioning mode. The first question is asked and the interviewee will naturally begin his or her presentation by answering it. The first question is usually broad enough so that the interviewee can respond easily. Often the interviewer sets the stage as follows: "Tell me about your education. Start with high school and mention your best courses, how you did, and what interested you and why."

This gives the applicant a lot of ground to cover and the applicant can choose an approach which feels comfortable. While this question seems to cover a lot of ground, it is useful because it serves as an introduction to the topic of educational background. Once the applicant is talking, the interviewer can begin to ask the structured questions which have been developed to yield information about the employee competences needed for the open job.

FIRST IMPRESSION ERROR

Many errors occur in the evaluation of interview data. These errors will be covered in Chapter 5. However, the interviewer must take care to avoid evaluation errors during the interview. If an error is committed during the interview, it could bias the type of data collected or the way the data are noted and remembered. A common error is to let first impressions have undue influence. The first thing an interviewer notices about someone is their appearance. While many applicants will dress for success when preparing for an interview, others may opt to be themselves and appear as they normally do. The point is that the interviewer should not be misled by appearances. An applicant who creates a strong first impression may be able to influence the final evaluation by this strong favorable feeling. The interviewer should recognize this as an emotional reaction. In some jobs, first impressions are a job-related competence factor. For most jobs, first impressions are not relevant. If it were relevant, a rating category, developed during preparation, would be available for subsequent evaluation.

If one notices that one has been affected by a strong first impression during an interview, the danger of making an error can be minimized; note the strong first impression and continue on with the interview. Do not let the strong first impression develop into a halo which will probably bias ratings on competence factors having nothing to do with it.

CONTRAST EFFECT AND SIMILARITY EFFECT

There are some additional errors which can throw off an interview. These errors crop up during interviews and during the subsequent evaluation process. The contrast effect has to do with applicants the interviewer has seen prior to the applicant now being seen. If the previous applicant, for example, was particularly well qualified, the interviewer may downgrade the present applicant because of this comparison. The comparison, incidentally, may be made on a subconscious level. Therefore, one must be attuned to one's emotions in order to pick up this reaction. To ignore it could lead to a rating in which the interviewer rates the applicant lower on competence-based rating scales than they may merit.

The contrast effect can work in the favorable direction too. If the previous applicant was weak, the present applicant may appear strong. This, too, could throw off ratings.

Another typical error that can occur during an interview is the similarity effect. This is simply the natural tendency to take a liking to those who are like us. In this case, the similarity may be to the interviewer or to the image projected by the organization. Typical issues where similarity may be a factor are age, appearance, and school affiliation. Again, this effect may not operate on a conscious level. One must be attuned to one's emotions in order to detect whether one is being swayed by the similarity effect. If one is, the way to counteract the effect is simply to stick to the interview plan. The plan is an objective approach which will yield sufficient data to make ratings. The final decision should follow from the ratings, not a gut feeling that an applicant is suited for the job.

INTERVIEWING DO'S AND DO NOT'S

Employment interviewing is an error prone process. The interviewer has biases which must be overcome in order to achieve objectivity. Also, there are errors which are specific to the interviewing process, namely, the first impression error, the similarity effect, and the contrast effect. In Chapter 1 and Chapter 7, some common interview errors are addressed. In Chapter 5, errors which are specific to the applicant rating process are explained. The reader will see that employment interviewing is like a two-sided coin. On one side are the do factors. These are things an interviewer is recommended to do in order to have an effective selection process. On the other side are the do not factors. There are pitfalls which the interviewer is cautioned to avoid. Committing any one of these errors could threaten the validity of the interview process.

TAKING NOTES

A major part of conducting an employment interview is the process of note taking. There are several reasons for taking notes, such as the following:

1. If one is seeing several applicants per day, one will find it hard to keep all the facts about each applicant in mind.
2. If one is very busy with other matters, one will not retain enough information about an applicant.
3. The idea of employment interviewing is to collect data for subsequent use in evaluation. If one does not take notes, the resulting data will be limited.
4. Interview notes are the basis for documenting the interview. As such, they should reflect job-related information conveyed to the interviewer by the applicant. No hint of bias should appear in the interview notes.

Some interviewers believe that taking notes will intimidate an applicant. This need not be so. The interviewer should ask the applicant for permission to take notes at the onset of the interview. The applicant will invariably give consent. If necessary, one may cite one of the reasons given in order to explain why one needs to take notes.

Interview notes are not a transcript of the interview. Rather, interview notes will be reflective of the preparation made for the interview. At the outset of the interview, the interviewer knows the areas in which he/she will make ratings later. The interviewer can, therefore, anticipate that numerous pieces of evidence will come forth during the interview which will be relevant to the rating categories. The interviewer will note these facts about the applicant as they occur. The most important thing to take notes on are the situation(s) described by the applicant, what the applicant did in the situation(s), and the outcome(s). These notes will be crucial in remembering the interview. Later, the interviewer can sort the facts into their appropriate categories, and they can be used to make several ratings. In order to believe that a rating is valid, an interviewer should have at least one solid basis for making the rating. A documented behavioral incident or behavioral intention given to an interviewer by an applicant is ideal for this purpose.

The interviewer should leave time at the end of the interview to develop complete notes on the behavior descriptions elicited from the applicant. This should be done immediately after the interview in order to retain as much material as possible. At this time the interviewer can link behavior descriptions with relevant competences.

The issue of negative information which is revealed by the applicant is a special situation in the employment interview. Applicants will reveal negative information about themselves. Although such behavior usually is kept from strangers, the interviewer has set the stage for an open and candid conversation. The result will be that applicants will share both positive and negative information about themselves. The interviewer does not alarm the interviewee by taking notes on a negative fact as soon as it has been shared with him/herself. The facts are kept in the back of the mind and are noted down at a later time when neutral or positive information is being revealed. This will allow the interviewer to maintain good rapport with the applicant.

After the interview, the interviewer will want to refine his/her notes and discard the ones on his/her notepad. The interviewer may also add notes that he/she has in memory. The interviewer tries to be as complete as possible. The interviewer sets aside some time after the interview for finalizing the notes. The interviewer will find that one forgets important material quickly after the interview has ended. The interviewer assures that the interview notes do not reflect any bias.

The time after the interview is good for noting observations the interviewer has made about the applicant. Oral communication skills and professional appearance are two things that lend themselves to this treatment. There will be other observations that one makes which are more subtle. If one has observed discrepancies in the applicant's presentation, one may have a basis for claiming that the applicant was exaggerating too much during the interview. If an applicant has let slip some clues about a negative attitude toward work, supervisors, coworkers, or an employee, one will note this after the interview. It is best to remain neutral during the interview when such slips occur. The interviewer's purpose is to encourage more comments. Afterwards, the interviewer will note what was observed.

If one is well prepared, one will see several clues to the applicant's real strengths and weaknesses. These clues are important because they represent in-depth information that can only be obtained by an interview. No one strength or weakness will dictate the final decision (with a few exceptions). One notes them down and incorporates them into the subsequent evaluation process.

Taking notes will benefit the interviewer. Each interviewer will find a method of taking notes which will be effective for him or her. While taking notes is important, the interviewer does not let note taking detract from the goal of an open conversational dialogue with the applicant. If one finds note taking to conflict with one's personal style, one can minimize it during the interview and complete the interview notes afterwards. Be sure to allow time for this activity.

BEHAVIORAL CLUES

Behavioral clues are a key to understanding an applicant. They abound, but interviewers must develop skill in using them. Much of the interview is determined by prior planning and consists of asking the planned questions. When dealing with clues, the process becomes more subtle.

The interviewer observes clues but does not reveal that they are being observed. The interviewer does not stop at the point of initial observance, however. A clue (i.e., a derogatory remark about corporate politics) can be used to probe in a way which could not have been anticipated by the interviewer prior to the interview. This must be done with considerable skill or the interviewee will be alarmed and may cease to be open. The use of clues is not a search for negative information. Rather clues point out areas of interest to the interviewer which coincide with the predetermined goal of the interview. For example, one is concerned with creativity. The interviewee states that he thinks his science teacher made the subject boring. The interviewer might ask the interviewee what he/she did to spice up his/her science course. The use of clues forces the interviewer into an evaluative posture. This is not the preferred focus during the interview, when the interviewer is trying to gather as much information as possible. The interviewer does not reveal his/her evaluation. The interviewer does not even let an evaluative tone slip into the tone of voice. The interviewer does not let evaluation cut off an intended line of questioning or curtail the interview unduly. The acquisition of clues during an interview guides the interviewer to new areas of probing and a deeper understanding of the applicant. Later, during evaluation, the interviewer will use the clues and additional information they lead to in the process of making ratings. Clues can also provide the basis for documenting interview ratings if they are in the form of behavior descriptions.

QUESTIONING TECHNIQUES

Questions are main components of the planned pattern of the interview. They serve the purpose of initiating and maintaining discussions of key areas of the applicant's background. The use of questions represents a big contrast to the use of clues. To use clues in an interview, one must be clever and analytical. To use a question, the interviewer must be prepared and skillful. The two approaches complement one another. The interviewer's ability to frame good questions appears more salient because the applicant sees only this part of the interviewer's craft.

The interview begins with open-end questions. This type of question is used to initiate discussion with the applicant. The reason why the interviewer uses open-end questions is that the interviewer wants the applicant to do most of the talking. The open-end question gives the applicant a place to start, a topic to address, and a blank slate on which to place his/her comments. The interviewer is in a position to listen, take notes, and direct the discussion.

Some open-end questions were illustrated in Chapter 3. The sample questions in that chapter contain many examples of open-end questions. In some cases, the term open-end question is a misnomer. What often suffices is a statement, such as, "Tell me about . . . " While technically not a question, this technique opens up a topic for the applicant to make comments. The applicants will respond with whatever information they believe is relevant.

The open-end question is accompanied by probes. If the applicant is giving useful information, there is no need to probe. However, most applicants can only go so far with an open-end question. The probes keep the conversation going. The interviewer might say "Tell me more . . . "; "In what way . . . "; "How did that come about?"; or, "Why did you . . . " The idea is to generate more discussion of a relevant topic.

Probing is generally an acceptable questioning technique. However, the interviewer must be careful not to begin framing new questions during the interview. The idea of structured interviews is to ask the same questions of each applicant. However, it is the author's view that to give up the probe question, as some structured interview techniques advocate, puts the interviewer at a disadvantage. The probe question allows the interviewer to deal with situations such as reticent applicants, applicants who may be covering up gaps in their record, and cases where good questioning technique will reveal much more about the applicant. There is support for probe questions from the leading theorists on structured interviewing. Motowidlo, Carter, Dunnette, Tippins, Werner, Burnett, and Vaughan (1992) have developed an approach to structured interviewing based on research studies they conducted. They call their approach the structured behavior interview. As part of their approach, they recommend the use of discretionary probing questions to obtain details of the situation, the interviewee's behavior in the situation, and the outcome of the behavior being described by the applicant. Such probes are called follow-up questions by Taylor and O'Driscoll (1995). They state that experienced interviewers develop follow-up questions during the interview. Follow-up questions can also be used to help the applicant focus on specific incidents, rather than responding with generalizations. Once that applicant realizes that the interviewer seeks detailed descriptions of behavior in specific situations, follow-up questions will become less relevant. Follow-up questions are also crucial in providing the interviewer additional details about a situation the applicant is describing. Open-ended, follow-up questions are most preferred.

With the exception of the broad questions which introduce broad topical areas, the interviewer asks one question at a time. This is a matter of good communication. If one asks too many questions at once, the applicant may become confused. Also, the interviewer may not receive answers to all questions unless one asks them one at a time.

There are some other communication issues as well. Questions should be carefully worded to avoid misunderstandings. Most interviewers can recall situations where the response obtained from someone in a conversation was totally different from what was expected. The respondent did not understand what was asked and was speaking in a manner which reflected his/her understanding, not ours. While this is acceptable in friendly conversations, it is bad form in an employment interview. It disrupts the concentration of both parties. It tends to dilute the serious atmosphere of the meeting. It conveys a bad impression to the interviewee. The interviewer must consider the wording of questions carefully. Of course, the questions developed before the interview will be easy to screen for clarity. If the interviewer forms probe questions during the interview, in response to information the interviewee has given, one must be sure the wording is clear.

Interviewers should distinguish between direct and indirect questions. The ideal approach to employment interviewing emphasizes the indirect question. For one thing, the interviewer does not want to tell the applicant what he/she expects to hear. The applicants' response should come from their own point of view. The interviewer will read the responses and later will evaluate them. The indirect approach is also less stressful. The applicants will not feel that they are failing the interview because they could not point to significant accomplishments in each area of their background. The indirect approach makes for a more comfortable conversational interview style. The interviewer may believe that such is not time efficient. Be prepared to spend an adequate amount of time to accommodate the indirect approach. It is the best approach and a good employment interview takes time to conduct.

What are some problems with direct questions? The yes–no question is not recommended. The conversation stops when the interviewee has answered yes or no. Then the interviewer must keep the interview going with another question. Before long, the interview has become an interrogation. The atmosphere of open exchange of information has broken down into the kind of alienated exchange one might engage in when applying for a driver's license. The yes–no question belongs on an application blank, not in the interview.

Direct questions may be perceived as antagonistic by the applicant. This is especially so if the answer they give reflects badly on them. Applicants would rather make their responses in such a way that anything negative is softened. The direct question demands a direct response and this may be uncomfortable for the applicant.

Direct questions may also tip the interviewer's hand. They may be leading questions. A leading question is one where the correct response is obvious to the applicant. Ninety-nine percent of applicants will respond with the correct answer to a leading question. It has nothing to do with honesty. It is common sense for an applicant to look good in an interview. Asking a leading question is a surefire way to evoke a distorted response from an applicant. Examples of leading questions might be the following:

- We're looking for self-starters. Are you a self-starter? Explain why.
- We believe in hard work here. How would you say your work performance can be rated? Why do you say this?
- We want people who aim to make a career in this industry. Is this your goal? Tell me more about it.

The indirect approach in employment interviewing is characterized by tact and skillful questioning. This approach may take a little longer but the payoff will be a more relaxed and more talkative applicant. Applicants prepare for the interview by developing ways of presenting themselves which have an optimal effect on the interviewer; the interviewer should remember that they practice also. The interviewer must get behind the prepared script of the applicant if insightful judgment about the applicant is to result. Questions should not be transparent. The applicant should not be led either. Trick questions will not only hurt the atmosphere of the interview but also consume a lot of energy on the part of the interviewer. The best bet is to provide a level playing field on which all applicants have the same conditions. The interviewer's edge will come from listening well and following up on clues which interest or alarm.

The main focus of questioning should be to elicit actual behavior which might be exhibited during a specific incident. This information (if valid) will give a basis to make predictions about the applicant's future behavior. It is true that people can and do change, but a good rule of thumb in employment interviewing is that behavior which the applicant has exhibited in the past is a good guide to how the applicant will behave in the future (Janz, 1989).

The behavioral intention question is a central part of employment interviewing. While behavioral intentions are not certain to be carried out in a new employee's future behavior, they are an important indication of how the applicant thinks. The responses to such questions throw light on an applicant's skills, knowledge, and abilities (as such, they are clues). The applicant may have rehearsed the answers to questions about previous experience. However, it is unlikely that the applicant will give a rehearsed answer to a behavioral intention question. Their responses will be indicators of their skill, knowledge, ability, and competence.

If one must ask tough questions, one saves them for the end of the interview. Sometimes there will still be gaps in the applicant's record near the close. One must get this information because it often reveals an important phase of the work or educational record. If the applicant has not supplied the information, the interviewer asks directly about what the applicant was doing during the time unaccounted for. The tone of the interview will change, but by that time the interviewer will have had sufficient time to observe the applicant. The end of the interview is also the time for tough questions, namely, Does the applicant possess some important minimum qualifications? Will the applicant relocate? or, What are the applicant's salary expectations? Do not hesitate to ask these questions because the responses may be crucial to the final decision.

This author's emphasis on questioning techniques stems from the fact that this is a key element in employment interviewing. The interviewer is expected to ask questions and let the applicant do the talking. Questions are both stimuli and control techniques. Regardless of how structured (or unstructured) the interview procedure, each applicant should receive consistent treatment. The resulting information given by the interviewee will be a reflection of the applicant's strength and weakness. A structured interview approach makes it more likely that each applicant will receive the same questions.

CONVERSATION STIMULATORS

Several interviewing techniques which will stimulate conversation are covered earlier in this chapter. Now, additional methods are covered. The material on establishing rapport is clearly intended to initiate an open, candid, complete description of an applicant's background. The various questioning techniques which are covered are also intended to stimulate conversation (and maintain rapport). Also, many applicants will be highly motivated by the opportunity to talk about their background, accomplishments, interests, and activities. The employment interview is a business meeting which has many built in stimuli to conversation for many people. Of course, there will be some people who are not talkative in an interview. These may include introverted individuals, people from family or social backgrounds which have left them ill prepared for the corporate world, and people who are new to the workforce.

An important skill for interviewers to learn is dealing with negative information. Some applicants will be aware that negative information is a red light to interviewers and will avoid mentioning anything negative about their background. There are many interviewing courses and books which will counsel job seekers not to reveal anything negative. On the other hand, there will be applicants who are naive about professional selection practices. These applicants

will be likely to be extremely candid about previous experience, both positive and negative. They will reveal that they flunked out of school, they were
fired from a job, they were caught violating the law, and so forth. The typical
applicant will be reluctant to reveal negative information but will nevertheless give a complete work history. Parts of their work history or educational
background may contain negative information which the applicant reveals in
the course of answering questions.

The basic procedure to follow when negative information is revealed in an
interview is to downplay the information. One can downplay the information
by asserting that it really is not bad at all, that it could happen to anyone, or
that it has happened to me, too. In fact, people with low self-esteem will present
themselves in a negative light even though they have very strong capabilities.
Downplaying the negatives in that case is a form of support to the interviewee.
In all cases, downplaying negative information has the effect of maintaining
a positive climate in the interview. It is a major goal of the interviewer to
maintain this positive climate so that effective communication will occur.

The probe is another important conversation stimulator. Since the interviewer is striving to get the applicant to do most of the talking, the interviewer's
role is to ask questions, maintain rapport, listen, and take notes. This does not
mean that the interviewer must remain silent. Probes allow one to maintain
his/her end of the conversation while also stimulating discussion of a point
about which one wants to hear more. An applicant may not be able to sense if
he/she has said enough about a topic or if they are focusing on a topic of importance to the job opening. A probe will indicate to the interviewee the
interviewer's interest in the topic of discussion. The probe will also direct the
applicant's remarks to aspects of the topic which have not yet been covered.
Those new aspects of the topic may reveal information that will allow the interviewer to tell how well the applicant did, how much complexity was involved, what the motivation of the applicant was in regard to the topic, and
many other facts which will help later during the evaluation of the information obtained in the interview.

A probe follows directly from the question which initiated discussion of a
particular topic. The following are some examples of how probes are developed. If the interviewer has asked an applicant a question about an important
decision he/she has made, the interviewer might probe with the question,
What factors influenced your decision. If the interviewer has asked a question about an experience in which the applicant had to work closely with others, the interviewer might probe with the question, How did it go? or, How
did you overcome any difficulties? If the interviewer has asked a question
about a project which the applicant initiated on his or her own, he/she might
probe with the question What else did you do? or, Why did you do it? Be careful
to avoid turning the probe into a leading question, however.

The mark of a professional interviewer is composure and the ability to
maintain a pleasant manner throughout all phases of the interview. One may

believe that this mark of professionalism is a natural interpersonal ability and that some people have it and some people do not. Actually interviewing skill can be cultivated, and with practice almost all interviewers will appear natural during the most stressful interview situations.

Some interviewing skills are verbal and some are nonverbal. Each skill is a finite gesture, but when the skills are combined and used in a dynamic interaction, they unite into a personal interview style. Skills will be examined one by one. These skills require practice and integration with the structure of the interview before they achieve the desired effect.

A basic interview skill is head nodding. This nonverbal gesture shows the interviewee that one is listening and that one understands what is being communicated. The interviewer tries to be nonevaluative when using this gesture. One does not want to lead the applicant. Rather, one wishes to encourage the applicant to continue the discussion of the current topic and to go into more depth.

Smiling or laughing (when appropriate) indicates that the interviewer enjoys the interviewee's company and that one is listening with interest. Another important nonverbal skill is maintaining eye contact. This indicates a sincere interest in the applicant. It is not necessary to maintain a steady gaze into the applicant's eyes. This may be too intense for some applicants to handle. The interviewer has several tasks which will require a break in eye contact. These include reference to a list of interview questions, taking notes, and adjusting one's posture in order to appear relaxed. A relaxed manner (such as leaning back in a chair) is an indication that one is willing to listen to the applicant. Leaning forward in a chair shows the applicant that one is interested in what he/she is saying and that one wants the applicant to continue talking about the topic being discussed.

There are also some verbal means of giving the applicant encouragement. It is important to interject a comment from time to time in order to hold up one's end of the conversation. A comment, such as, "Uh-huh", "I see", or "I understand" will indicate that one is listening and is interested in what the applicant is saying. If one wishes the applicant to say more, one could utilize supportive comments and praise. This is a way of recognizing an accomplishment. One should not be evaluative when one praises the applicant. This is merely another technique for stimulating conversation and should not imply anything about one's subsequent ratings.

Just as one cultivates a pleasant manner by one's nonverbal gestures, one's pace and style will create a pleasant climate for communication. The interviewer is polite to the applicant. This does not mean the interviewer must be formal at all times. Polite treatment of the applicant shows respect for him/her as a person. The interviewer does not rush through the interview. Rushing will convey that the interview is not the interviewer's highest priority. The interviewer speaks in a pleasant tone of voice. The interviewer tries not to appear nervous during the interview. An employment interviewer always avoids interruptions to the interview. This includes telephone calls which interrupt the interview.

The interviewer tries to be nonevaluative in his/her comments. While one may not agree with the applicant, one gives him/her a positive response. The objective is to have the applicant continue talking, and agreeing with the applicant will have that effect. The interviewer resists the temptation to give advice to the applicant. Often giving advice to the applicant will be a turnoff. It may indicate a premature decision on the interviewer's part that the applicant is not suitable. It may be patronizing (the interviewer is offering his/her opinion based on a better perspective than the applicant has). It may be inappropriate or poor judgment because one does not have all the facts. The applicant is looking for a job, not the interviewer's opinion.

A key conversation stimulator is reflection. This technique is used by counselors when they are trying to listen to their clients. The interviewer must be tuned in to the emotional content of the applicant's comments. If the interviewer is in touch with the emotional state of the applicant and communicates that understanding to the applicant, the applicant will be encouraged to talk more about the topic under discussion. Often the additional comments of the interviewee will provide the depth needed for the interviewer to make an effective evaluation of the applicant at a later time.

To illustrate reflection, one can assume the applicant is discussing how he/she achieved a sales quota in a direct selling situation, such as the following:

APPLICANT: I had a really tough sales quota to meet. If I made the quota, it would mean that I would be one of the leading sales people. I would also qualify for a sales bonus.

INTERVIEWER: You were really proud to be one of the leading salespeople and of the recognition it would bring you.

APPLICANT: That's right. It was a tremendously exciting feeling. The reason I was able to meet the quota was that I was putting in seventy-hour weeks with no Saturdays off. It was a sacrifice, but that's the way I am in a competitive sales situation.

Note that the interviewer reflected back the emotional content of the applicant's comments. The interviewer is not merely paraphrasing the applicant's comments. The applicant replies by filling in information on how he/she accomplished his sales and why he/she put so much effort into this task. Reflection only works when the interviewer is tuned in emotionally. The interviewer should not attempt to use it unless the interviewer believes he/she understands the applicant at this level.

It should go without saying that listening is an important interviewing skill. When one is listening, one will pick up clues from the applicant which will help one to evaluate the applicant. Also, the applicant will sense one's empathy and will be inclined to comment in depth. If the applicant senses that one is not listening (due to distractions, other pressing matters on one's mind, or premature evaluation leading to disinterest on the interviewer's part) the applicant will be turned off, and one will not get the in-depth information needed to make an evaluation.

Another basic conversation stimulator is summarizing. As the interview goes on, one forms an understanding of what the applicant is saying. The interviewer should not forget that this is his/her understanding. The applicant may not have been saying exactly what the interviewer believes he/she was saying. If one summarizes one's understanding of what the applicant was saying, one will give the applicant a chance to correct any misunderstanding. Also, the interviewer will be showing the applicant that there are some things he/she has not told the interviewer. The applicant will then make additional comments in order to give the complete picture.

Sometimes, a predetermined question will not yield the kind of information needed in order to make a selection decision. One does not abandon a line of questioning too soon. Often alternative questions will get the information one is seeking. The interviewer rewords the original question. He/she develops an entirely new question. The interviewer tries to come at the question from a fresh and original point of view. The use of alternative questions will often yield useful information in an interview.

The topic of the need for politeness is considered again from a new angle. The interviewer must not be impolite. Impoliteness is not only rude it is also a turnoff. What does the author mean by impoliteness? In an employment interview, the issue is interruption of the applicant, cross-examination of the applicant (the third degree treatment used by police interrogators) changing the subject abruptly (before the applicant has finished his/her comments) criticizing the applicant, arguing with the applicant, or disagreeing with the applicant. While these kinds of messages may be appropriate in some business meetings, they are dysfunctional in an employment interview. In the heat of an interview, one may be tempted to interject a comment but the interviewer should hold back when possible. While the interviewer may be correct from an objective point of view, he/she will be inhibiting the comments of the interviewee. This is contrary to the goal of the interviewer: to draw out the applicant in as much depth as possible.

CONTROL

An important issue at the onset of an interview is control. The interviewer always maintains control. This includes what topic is being discussed, keeping the discussion on track, how much time is allotted to each topic, avoiding digressions, backtracking to gain clarity, and keeping to the planned interview schedule. Some applicants will try to wrest control from the interviewer. The appropriate response by the interviewer is to guide the conversation back on track. The interviewer does this in a way that permits the maintenance of rapport.

The employment interviewer must gain control of the interview and must retain control throughout the interview. The employment interview is often time constrained. An employment interviewer will see many candidates during a day and scheduling demands may limit interview duration. A manager interviewing a prospective employee must find the time in a busy schedule. It is difficult for some managers to free up one hour of uninterrupted time for each job applicant. Therefore, the interviewer must maximize the time spent with each applicant. Having a planned interview schedule is one way of maximizing the time. Careful preparation is another. Maintaining control assumes that all that the interviewer intended to do during the interview actually comes to pass.

When one says control one means that the interviewer actively utilizes interviewing skill in conducting the interview. One may note that some of the procedures used to control the interview seem to conflict with interviewing practices discussed. This need not be the case. The interviewer must be able to sense when he/she is losing control. This may occur when an applicant rambles on about a topic which is of minor importance. It may occur when an applicant does not respond to questions because he/she is seeking to dominate the interview by introducing another agenda. It may occur because an applicant is exaggerating his/her qualifications and is not giving concrete behavioral evidence to describe work experience or education. Some applicants are naturally aggressive and others see aggressiveness as a plus and try to portray themselves as such. Some applicants are not good communicators and find it hard to stay on track during a structured or patterned interview. Interviewers should not hesitate to actively maintain control. Maintaining control is simply an element in the process of employment interviewing which assumes that the process will be standardized and that each applicant has the same treatment.

Typically, the pace of the interview is determined by the planned interview schedule (i.e., steps to be followed, questions to be asked). Applicants vary widely in the way they react to interview questions. This is one reason why the interview is an effective selection procedure. This variance also could lead to some applicants taking more time than is available because of talkativeness, extensive background, or the applicant's own interview strategy and some applicants not taking enough time because of shyness, lack of experience, or poor communication skills. One aspect of control is assuming that each applicant receives a consistent interview. Since interviewers will compare applicants and select the best, the interviewer wants to be able to make comparisons among people who have responded to the same stimuli.

Another aspect of control is keeping the interview on track. The employment interview has a format which is similar from company to company and region to region. It is this similarity which allows the development of interviewing skills and interviewing techniques. Many applicants are also aware of the typical features of the interview. This makes the process smooth most of the time. Some applicants are not aware of the employment interviewing process or actively try to disrupt the process or preempt it for their own advantage. It is these applicants who need to receive active attempts by the interviewer to maintain control.

The most common form of maintaining control is for the interviewer to steer the conversation. While in most cases the interviewer will not have to interrupt the applicant, maintaining control may require an abrupt change of course. The interviewer indicates this change of course with skill, tact, and politeness. It is appropriate to mention that one thinks the current topic has been adequately covered and that one would like to move ahead. It is also appropriate to remind the interviewee of the planned schedule. For example, some applicants will ask questions about the job content at the beginning of the interview. Since the interviewer wants all applicants to respond to a similar job description when answering questions, the interviewer should remind the applicant that he/she will have a chance to ask questions at the end of the interview. Then one should proceed with the planned interview schedule.

Some applicants tend to wander. They start embellishing their background and do not respond to the question asked of them. They give a preplanned response which really doesn't answer the question. They are not focused communicators and switch from subject to subject, becoming vague and unclear in the process. These applicants need gentle (and persistent) help to stay on track.

Summarizing is also a control technique. If an applicant is going on too long about a particular topic, a summary indicates that the interviewer would like to draw to a close and start on a new topic.

Voice tone can be a control element. Most of the time the interviewer will maintain a pleasant tone in order to provide a positive climate for communication. Sometimes, however, voice tone will become formal. This should indicate to the applicant that one is telling him/her something which the interviewer expects they will understand in order to have a successful interview.

Remember that the applicant should do most of the talking. At least sixty percent (and ideally eighty percent) of the interview will be comments from the applicant. One must exercise control in order to achieve the desired talk ratio.

DEALING WITH SILENCE

Sometimes during an interview, there will be an unnatural silence. Since the interviewer is trying to create a pleasant conversational atmosphere in the interview, the silence will be unwelcome. It reminds the interviewer and the applicant of the fact that a selection decision is the outcome of each interview. When a silence develops, it is tempting for the interviewer to break the silence. The interviewer wants to jump in and speak in order to maintain that pleasant atmosphere which has been created. It is a mistake, however, for the interviewer to break the silence. The period of silence is also felt as pressure by the applicant. The applicant wants to create a positive impression and to keep the ball rolling from there. The applicant will perceive a period of silence as awkwardness, which they are seeking to avoid. Generally, if the interviewer sits in a composed manner, the applicant will break the silence. It becomes a control issue. By remaining composed, the interviewer maintains control. The information the applicant gives when he/she breaks the silence may be helpful in getting an in-depth view of the topic under discussion, since the applicant will have had time to gather thoughts on the topic.

If the silence goes on too long, the interviewer may want to make a comment in order to break the tension.

CLOSING THE INTERVIEW

As the interviewer comes to the end of the interview, he/she will take questions from the applicant and provide additional information about the job and the organization. There is a temptation to make the organization look desirable to desirable applicants. This is not a good procedure in an employment interview, and it is more likely to occur in a recruiting interview. Actually, a well-conducted employment interview presents a very positive image for the organization. When an applicant inquires about the job and the organization , it is best to be as specific as possible. Describe the job and the company realistically using the material obtained during the preparation process. If an applicant does not have strong qualifications, do not abruptly terminate the interview. However, the interviewer may take less time describing the job and company for such applicants.

The interviewer can ask the applicant if he/she has anything to add which has not already been covered. This is a communication technique which assumes that the applicant has a chance to mention information which the interviewer did not specifically elicit by planned questions.

The interviewer tells the applicant the next steps in the employment process. It not appropriate to give a decision during the interview. It is also inappropriate to telegraph one's feelings about the applicant's chances. It is helpful to the applicant to inform him/her of when the decision will be made and some of the steps which will be taken before the decision is made.

The interviewer thanks the applicant for his/her time. The interviewer escorts the applicant out of his/her office. The interviewer should remember to leave some time after the interview to complete the interview notes. The close of the interview is the interviewer's prerogative. The applicant will keep talking until the interviewer signals the end of the interview. The signal does not have to be explicit. The applicant will usually see very clearly when the end occurs. If necessary, one can make the end explicit.

CASE STUDY: EXAMPLE OF
AN EMPLOYMENT INTERVIEW

In order to illustrate some of these principles, an example is provided. The first step will be to examine the applicant's resumé. A hypothetical applicant, Sally Armstrong, is used. She is applying for the assistant manager position which was described in Chapter 3.

A transcript of a hypothetical interview between Ann Jones, manager of a retail chain store, and Sally Armstrong is presented. Naturally, all the elements of employment interviewing which have been explored cannot be contained in one example. The purpose of the example is to show how a competence-based structured interview looks. In Chapter 5, the data provided by this interview are rated for the purpose of demonstrating the evaluation process.

Applicant's Resumé

SALLY M. ARMSTRONG
14 Fieldstone Road   Southington, MA 01462   (617) 357–9211

OBJECTIVE

An assistant manager position in a growing fashion retail store.

EDUCATION

Stanhope High School   Stanhope, PA
Academic Program Graduate

A. A. in Fashion Merchandising, May 1988
Lee Community College   133 Main Street, Westville, MA 01463
Honors: Dean's List student

COURSE WORK

Marketing course, involving display techniques, pricing policy, advertising, how to sell to retail shoppers, and so forth. Retail Management Information Systems, involved getting point of purchase information to buyers, designing and operating re-order and stock systems, and analyzing sales data.

WORK EXPERIENCE

Summers 1983–1985: counter help at McDonalds restaurant, Stanhope, PA. Responsible for customer service, cleanup, and cash handling.

Summer, 1986: Clothes Workshop, Sales Assistant, ladies' fashions.

January 1985 to present: The Clothes Workshop, Inc.: Salesperson. Position duties included working the cash desk, handling layaways, record keeping, creating merchandise displays, ticketing, markdowns, inventory, enforcing shoplifting security, guiding and counseling customers on purchases, and opening and closing store.

PROFESSIONAL ASSOCIATIONS

American Marketing Association

COLLEGE AND COMMUNITY ACTIVITIES

Treasurer of Lee Community College Fashion Merchandising Association, September 1986 to May 1988. Volunteer at Stanhope Hospital, three to five hours per week spent with patients, doing errands, and so forth. Became leader of this volunteer organization.

REFERENCES

Furnished upon request.

STRUCTURED INTERVIEW TRANSCRIPT

ANN JONES: Good morning, Sally. How are you today?

SALLY ARMSTRONG: Hello, Ms. Jones. I'm fine, thank you.

ANN: Did you have any trouble finding my office? Sometimes people have trouble locating me, tucked away back here in the rear of the store.

SALLY: Well, actually, I have been a customer here several times so I kind of know my way around. One of your sales people directed me back here to the office.

ANN: I'm glad you could meet with me. We are looking for a person to be assistant manager. We have an excellent growth situation here at Lauren's Fashions, and we are looking for experienced people to help maintain that growth. The position reports to the store manager. Since we are open ten hours a day, the store manager needs an assistant to help run the store. In addition we look at assistant managers as having potential to move up rapidly to the store manager job. With that in mind, I would like to ask you some questions about your background. After I finish exploring your background in detail, there will be a chance for you to ask questions. Also, I will be taking notes during the interview. Do you mind?

SALLY: Not at all. I am familiar with the position and I would be happy to fill you in on relevant experience which I have had.

ANN: Now let's go ahead to explore your interest in fashion. Explain to me your knowledge of fashion trends.

SALLY: Ever since I was young I was interested in fashion. I have been an avid reader of fashion magazines. The public library is a good place to keep up with these publications when you're a student. I would have a lot of animated conversations with my friends about fashion. Also, I have always attended fashion shows when they were held in my area.

ANN: Could you tell me about some of your perceptions about the current fashion?

SALLY: Well yes . . . . I've been following the new styles from the Japanese designers. I really like the full-sleeve effect. It does a lot for women of all sizes. I'm also into the sweater look. You know sweaters are in this year. So many are available from Italy, China, and other countries around the world.

ANN: I always like to hear about fashion trends. It's so important to keep up. I see on your resumé that you have retail sales experience. Could you tell me about your sales experiences on your job?

SALLY: Sure. We were on salary but there were prizes for the best sales people. So we were always trying to make the sale. Greeting the customers was mandatory. But whenever I had the time I approached the customer, asked what she was looking for, and guided her to some attractive merchandise. My company had organized sales training meetings. A trainer would come in and show us the best way to sell to our customers. I tried to use the recommended approach whenever possible. Sometimes a customer just wanted to look. If I detected that a customer wanted some help, I would make suggestions about styles which I thought would be suitable. Women customers were easier to deal with. Once a few items had been identified I could accompany the customer into the back rooms, where try-ons are done. Once a customer starts to try on merchandise, they are much more likely to make a purchase. Once the basic purchase decision has been made, the sales person can suggest add-on purchases.

ANN: Can you describe how your sales performance was evaluated?

SALLY: Since we were on salary, we had no quotas. If you wanted to be a full-time employee, however, you had to be among the top sellers in the store. I was full-time during the summer, for several years, so I was always working on my sales. We kept records and the store manager knew who the better sales people were at all times.

ANN: You see a customer come into the store. Tell me how you would conduct a sales transaction. What would you do in this situation? Be sure to include all the details of the transaction that you can anticipate.

SALLY: I approach a customer with a big smile on my face. I look directly at them, make eye contact, and say, Hello! From the customer's reaction, I can usually judge if the customer would like some assistance. If the reaction is positive, I ask the customer what she is shopping for at the shop. The customer will typically indicate a category of merchandise. Let's say the customer is looking for a pair of Bermuda shorts. I would invite the customer to look at our collection of shorts, escort the customer to the rack, and allow the customer to look at the merchandise at her leisure. After a few minutes, I will choose some shorts from the rack and show them to the customer. The customer will usually indicate what is more or less preferable. In order to move the sale along, I will suggest going to the fitting room to try on two or three pairs of shorts. The best time to close the sale is after a try-on. I will always try to close a sale and then suggest some accessories to add to the outfit. However, I do not rush the customer.

ANN: In your present position, how do you relate interpersonally to customers, associates, and managers at the store?

SALLY: I try to become a member of the team at a store where I work. I consider my relationship with coworkers to be very important. If we all get along and cooperate, the store will have a good atmosphere. I think a customer prefers to shop in a store with a friendly sales staff which cooperates. I try to be a good team member. In my previous job, I liked the people I worked with. Our manager encouraged a team spirit, and although we all tried to be the best, we did it in a way that was fun, too. Going to work was always okay because you knew the others so well and enjoyed the time you spent with them. It certainly was good for us to be friendly, and I think the manager gets credit for encouraging it. Of course, I follow all the store rules, and I do not let friendship interfere with my job. I like working for a manager who runs an efficient store. The store should provide an opportunity for associates to interact with one another in order to develop teamwork. A store which prevents interaction with other associates and with customers is too impersonal for me.

ANN: Imagine an empty store window in our shop. What would you do in this situation?

SALLY: My preferred approach to window design is to show complete outfits. I like to design a mannequin with a bottom, say a skirt, a top, say a shirt, a sweater over the shirt, and accessories, say a scarf around the neck. This gives the customer an idea of a complete look using the current fashions and colors. Of course, a series of similar mannequins each featuring a different color scheme is most effective.

ANN: I see in your previous job you did layaways. Could you describe the procedures you used?

SALLY: After I had been at the store for a while, I was able to work the cash desk and handle layaways. The cashier did the paper work but I was asked to assist in keeping records. The store encouraged layaways so at certain times we had extensive inventories and records to keep.

ANN: Have you handled shoplifting incidents in the past?

SALLY: Yes, I have.

ANN: Please describe a situation you experienced which involved shoplifting.

SALLY: Well, I have always been vigilant about shoplifters. Some customers resent our keeping an eye on the merchandise but if you don't it will disappear. People are not afraid to try to shoplift. I guess they didn't think we would prosecute. They were wrong, but it was very stressful to accuse someone. You never knew how they would react.

ANN: Could you describe a specific situation?

SALLY: Actually, my boss usually deals with those situations.

ANN: Let's go on to your school record. What are some courses you've taken which would help in the assistant manager position?

SALLY: I was a Fashion Merchandising major. A very helpful course was Retail Merchandising. Our instructor had a lot of retail experience so we got a good background in display techniques, how to sell to retail shoppers, pricing policy, and advertising. The course was very practical, and since I was also working, I was able to apply my knowledge right away. Another helpful course was Retail Management Information Systems. So much store activity today focuses on getting point of purchase information to the buyers. It's possible to reorder just as the season is getting under way and have new stock of the best-selling items shipped by air from Hong Kong before the season is over. That really can boost sales. We learned how to design and operate such systems as well as how to analyze sales data.

ANN: What was your high school and college grade point average?

SALLY: Well, I was a B student in high school. In college, I ran a 3.0 grade point average.

ANN: Please tell me about the vision you have for your career in retailing?

SALLY: If I am going to make retailing my career, I want to try to get to the top. Management is the way to show you have ability. I know I can get along well with coworkers and customers. I want a chance to show I can get results as well. I hope to do so well as an assistant manager that you will promote me to a higher position of responsibility. Also, in a managerial position I can earn some money. I would like to get an apartment of my own and become financially independent now that school is over. Long term, I would like to use my knowledge of fashion merchandising to go to a major city and get involved with merchandising.

ANN: You have a solid foundation for a career in retailing. You should be aware that our successful store managers often have a chance to get into buying positions in the home office.

SALLY: That sounds great. I would like to have a lot more store management experience before considering an office job, however.

ANN: You will find that Lauren's Fashions will allow you to advance and will pay you well if you succeed. I'm not going to promise anything, but we are large enough to be able to provide opportunities for our most talented employees. I have your application, and I will be considering it in the next week or so. Are there any questions before we end?

SALLY: Do you have any literature about the company?

ANN: Oh, I was about to give you this. Here is some additional information about the chain. Thanks for coming in. I will be in touch.

SALLY: Nice to meet you. I hope to hear from you soon about the job. It sounds very interesting.

The model interview included in this chapter continues the case study begun in Chapter 3. The reader can now see how the extensive preparation for the interview pays off. The interviewer can quickly get to the points necessary to determine if the applicant has the needed competence to perform at a high level in the open position.

Chapter Five

Evaluation of Applicants

The evaluation process completes the cycle began when the interviewer engaged in preparing for the interview. At that time all one had was information on the job and some rudimentary information about applicants. The information about the job was the mainstay. It consisted of tasks, responsibilities, knowledge requirements, skill requirements, ability requirements, and competence factors. The employee competence factors (taken together) represent an abstract of the job. Now one changes the mind-set. Now the employee competence factors become the basis for rating applicants for the job.

RECAPITULATION OF THE COMPETENCE-BASED EMPLOYMENT INTERVIEW MODEL

Now that the evaluation interview data are the issue, it will be helpful to review the model in schematic form. The model depicted in Figure 5.1 includes the basic steps in the selection process. The evaluation step is pictured as a series of ratings that the interviewer makes as the basis for the final selection decision. The reader will see that the process returns to the rigor first introduced in the preparation phase. The ratings are made on scales based on the competence factors originally developed by position analysis. In addition to ratings on each competence factor, a summary rating is made. A worksheet is suggested for combining the ratings of multiple interviewers. The final selection decision is made based on interview ratings as well as other evaluative matters deemed crucial by the employer.

A key part of competence-based structured interviewing is the ability to collect data which will allow completion of the subsequent evaluation. For instance, the applicant will come prepared to give the interviewer a chronological educational background and work history. The applicants may also have

Figure 5.1
Competence-Based Structured Interviewing Process—Evaluation of Applicants

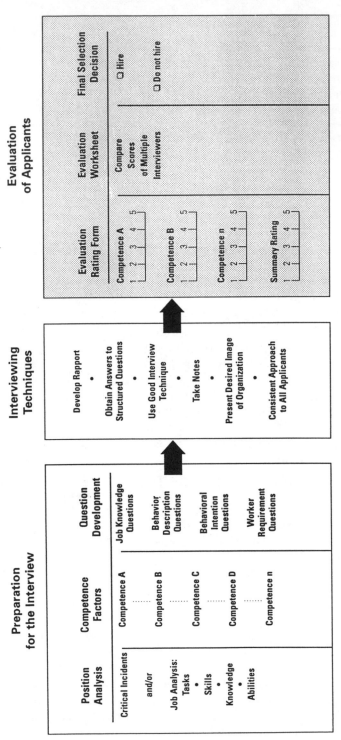

prepared promotional messages which bring out their best side. It may be appropriate to interrupt the applicant's presentation if it is off track or if it is so polished that the interviewer feels he/she is not getting all the facts. On the other hand, most of the data one gets will be in the form the applicant wishes to package and present to the interviewer. During the evaluation phase the interviewer processes the information, makes ratings from it, and develops a judgment about the applicant's chances of performing at a high level in the open position. In other words, that neat presentation the applicant made of himself/herself must be converted to an evaluation of the applicant's competence. Since the interview does not deal exclusively with applicant competence, part of the evaluation process is to extract evidence of applicant competence from the notes of the interview or one's memory of the interview.

This procedure should make clear why it is important to take notes during the interview. If one is seeing many applicants or is very busy, one may not have all the data one needs to make an evaluation when that time comes. The best time to complete the evaluation is soon after the interview has ended. One goes over the interview notes as soon after the interview ends as possible to make sure they are complete.

During the evaluation the interviewer will peruse notes looking for clues, behavior, and credentials—what a person actually has done. The reader should recall that the employee competence factors originally led to questions. During the interview the interviewer collected relevant information. After the interview this information is input for ratings and documentation of the ratings. This is a demanding process. One may not have enough information to make ratings on all the competence factors which were identified. It is best in that case not to make a rating on a scale where one believes one has no information. On the other hand, good preparation and good interviewing skill will assure that the interviewer has the information needed. If one intends to conduct a validation of the interview process at a later time, it is essential that one be able to make ratings on all the relevant competence factors.

USE OF COMPETENCE FACTORS IN EVALUATION

Employee competence factors provide a frame of reference, an evaluation yardstick, or a series of evaluation benchmarks against which one can evaluate (rate) the applicant's qualifications. Prior to evaluation, the interviewer should review definitions of employee competence previously determined to be relevant to the open position. If, for example, one is chiefly interested in such factors as adaptability, dependability, or willingness to work hard, one should continually have these factors in mind when evaluating recollections and notes on the interview. Hence, one will be more likely to pick up on significant clues and interpret them in relation to the proper selection standards.

Most researchers recommend that a scoring protocol be developed before the interview. A scoring protocol will advise interviewers what are the expected responses to interview questions. A scoring protocol can be simple or complex. The simple type will indicate what is a favorable or an unfavorable comment by an interviewee. Such protocols will guide the interviewer, who still exercises considerable judgment in making ratings. A complex protocol will try to anticipate every possible response and may also indicate how to rate each response. Such a complex scoring protocol is possible when there are large numbers of applicants on a regular basis for the same position.

Employee competence factors developed before the interview become rating scales in evaluation. Therefore skills, knowledge, abilities, and competence must be considered in a new light. This new focus deals with the individual nature of the interview data. In the interview, one hears about and observes work and related experience, education and training, abilities, motivation and personality traits, and physical qualifications. In order to make ratings in evaluative categories, the interview data must be sorted. This process of sorting (information processing in a judgmental manner) may be seen as several steps, such as the following:

1. Obtain data on applicants
2. Match clues, facts, credentials, behavior, and behavior intentions to relevant rating scales (a behavioral incident mentioned by an applicant may apply to several rating scales)
3. Try to have several bits of information for each rating scale, in order to make the best rating possible

WEIGHTING COMPETENCE FACTORS

In the job analysis or critical incident analysis conducted prior to the interview, there is often evidence that some factors are more important than others in determining effective job performance. On the Competence Model Worksheet, Appendix 3.C codes are provided to assess how important each competence factor is for job success. A code of one indicates slight importance for job success. A code of two indicates moderate importance for job success. A code of three indicates extreme importance for job success. In developing a summary rating for an applicant, these success factor codes can be used to weight competence factors. The summary rating becomes a weighted average where the weights are the success factor codes or other weights deemed appropriate by the interviewer.

FINAL SELECTION DECISION

In making a final decision, the organization may also consider knockout factors (musts), other interviewers' ratings (multiple interviews), test scores (if available), weights of the various competence factors (the most important competence factors are given greater weight in computing an average rating score), strengths versus weaknesses (compensatory model of evaluation), and overall ratings. In order to make a final selection decision, all the applicants for the job are compared to a standard. Applicants are compared to a company standard (i.e., competences required by the job). Also, the interviewer may use previous interviewing experience to develop a personal standard (e.g., previous successful hires or the best applicants he/she has ever seen).

There are several aspects of evaluation which are more common sense than technical. For example, if one does not have an adequate number of applicants for a job one may not be in a position to make a meaningful selection. If there are too few applicants for the job, choosing the best among them may not be a meaningful decision. This is a shortcut which may eliminate the benefits of the selection model. It is quite possible that none of the applicants has the desired competence. In this case the appropriate action is to continue recruiting until suitable applicants are found. Also, if the interview time with an applicant is too short, the interviewer cannot use an in-depth system such as the one recommended in this book. Some methods of selection are rigorously quantitative. There may be a highly valid test for a job which surpasses any other selection procedure for predicting job success. In that case the interview would be deemphasized, and the test score would be the major selection criterion. Having such a test is rare in today's employment environment. The employment interview is the dominant selection procedure by far in the United States and abroad.

THE USE OF CLUES

A basic concept to keep in mind during evaluation is that past work behavior is the best predictor of future work behavior (Janz, 1989). This statement is accurate because people tend to be consistent in their work behavior. It is because of this consistency that employment interviewing is a valuable employment procedure. It is the most suitable method for obtaining details about an applicant's past work-related behavior. Remember that the focus is always on behavior. The interview allows one to get to the story behind the story. The selection procedures recommended in this book allow the applicants to tell their story in their own words and in a comfortable conversational manner. Meanwhile, the interviewer's eyes and ears are open and are recording information about behavior in all its diverse forms, namely accomplishments, attitudes, values, beliefs, failures, goals, motivations, personality, interests, skills, knowledge, and intelligence. The interviewer is also alert for errors of omission and will probe to fill in any gaps in the applicant's record. If one gathers enough information to make a sound evaluation, one will have mapped a pattern of behavior which is likely to be repeated in the future.

A brief review of the use of clues, a topic covered earlier, is helpful here. Clues must be interpreted as soon as they are secured (i.e., during the interview). Clues are elements or fragments of an interviewee's behavior (past or present) which can lead to the interpretation of broader behavioral patterns. One can assess an interviewee's capability on a particular competence factor through the interpretation of several clues which apply to such a specification. Clues play a two-fold purpose. During the interview itself the evaluative posture of the interviewer is suppressed. The interviewer tries to appear nonjudgmental at all times. Nevertheless, the interviewer is always conducting an evaluation of a tactical nature. A clue which comes up during the interview may lead the interviewer to pose probe questions to uncover more information about behavior related to a competence factor. If a clue raises doubts, these must be dealt with before the interview concludes. For example, if planning and organizing is an important skill in a target job the clue *met all deadlines* would be positive evidence. On the other hand, the clue *stayed up all night studying for exams* might prompt further investigation during the interview (e.g., a probe about how the applicant organized his/her latest project).

Clues are often very subtle behaviors and are difficult to detect. Clues may stem from slight nuances in meaning (such as emphasizing or glossing over a fact), or they may originate in changes in vocal inflection, facial expression, or gestures which tip the interviewer that a significant behavior is being observed or related. Additional sources of clues are pauses or gaps in the applicant's conversation, any asides or other casual or parenthetical remarks he/she may make, any qualifications which he/she may introduce in the discussion, or any omissions or inconsistencies which may be observed in any part of the applicant's story. Since an interview reveals only fragments of a person's behavior, clues must be viewed as an indication of the need for further investigation. After the interview, clues are bits of evidence but one clue alone should not be the basis of an important rating or selection decision (especially if it is a piece of negative information which appears early in an interview). Since the interpretation of clues is an interpretive process, one must be alert to the possible errors which may occur in any rating process. The interviewer does not become so involved in the pursuit of a clue that he/she arouses an interviewee's suspicions. The applicants may become resentful if they feel the interviewer is sizing them up or putting them on the spot.

MAKING RATINGS

The rating scale can be made simple or complex depending on the need for subsequent data processing. If one were going to do a quantitative analysis of applicants, or an evaluation of the interviewing process, one would want to have an ordinal scale (five points for each scale). If one is simply comparing three or four job applicants, a three-point scale is adequate. Three points is a handy scale because it allows the interviewer to rate an applicant below-average, average, or above average on each scale. A rating scale must have a clear title in order to be useful. The title used for the employee competence factors will usually serve very well as the title of a rating scale. Developing a rating scale in this manner will ensure that one is using job-related procedures for selection of employees.

A way of bringing closure to the evaluation process is the completion of a rating form. Ratings may be made using several types of scales. An evaluation rating form consisting of five-point scales is generally recommended. The scale anchors are the following: lacks qualification, below average, average, above average, and highly competent. A blank evaluation rating form is included in this chapter as Appendix 5.A. The reader will note that in addition to the rating scale there is also space for documentation.

In documenting a rating the interviewer is distilling the written and mental notes made during the interview. These notes are for use during the interview process and are usually destroyed after a decision is made. The evaluation rating sheet, however, should be retained in company records, so the documentation included must be strictly job related. The best form of documentation is actual behavior of the applicant as revealed on the application, resumé, or in discussion during the interview. Preferably, this behavior will consist of a specific behavioral incident related to the interviewer by the applicant. If so, documentation would include the context of the incident (the situation), the behavior of the applicant during the incident, and the outcome of the incident. The behavior will clearly indicate the basis for a rating.

Taylor and O'Driscoll (1995) suggest that ratings should be made on the following basis: (1) how relevant behavioral descriptions offered by the applicant are to those that are faced by job incumbents; (2) how effective the applicant's behavior was in the situation; (3) how close the applicant's behavior was to the desired competence factor; (4) the number of behavior descriptions offered by the candidate for each competence factor (the more the better); and (5) the recency of the behavior descriptions offered by the applicant. The more relevant the applicant's behavior description is to the open position, the more confident the interviewer can be in his/her rating of the candidate. Also, the interviewer seeks to determine if the behavior the applicant describes has led to effective outcomes. This is also considered when rating the applicant.

While quotes from the applicant form the basis for documentation, typically the interviewer will add his/her insight to what the applicant has said. Whereas during the interview notes tend to be factual and descriptive of behavior, the documentation made on the evaluation rating sheet is more interpretive. For example, the following interpretive comment might summarize a high rating on a competence factor such as energy: "The fact that the applicant worked ten to twelve hours per day over a three-year period for the XYZ Company reveals a high level of energy." In general the remarks summarizing a rating will be interpretive, although it is advisable to include supporting information of a factual nature whenever possible. A single example of an applicant's behavior may be evidence of more than one competence factor. In that case the documentation of several ratings may be similar.

A competence evaluation documentation guide is included as Appendix 5.B of this chapter. In the guide, one will find numerous examples of behaviors which could be used in documenting interviewee behavior on the evaluation rating form. Naturally, the documentation for each type of job will be unique.

Occasionally there will be interviews in which one cannot obtain enough information to complete all the rating scales. This should not impair one's ability to make a selection decision, however. One makes ratings only on those scales for which there is sufficient data. Normally one will want at least two clues, pieces of behavioral evidence, credentials, behavioral intentions, or facts to back up a rating. If one has a strong basis to make a rating based on less data, one should not hesitate to do so.

It is helpful to write a summary when one has completed all the rating scales. Things to emphasize in the summary are applicant strengths, weaknesses, ratings on key (heavily weighted) scales, ratings about which one has the most confidence, and areas of doubt about the applicant's likelihood of long-term success on the job. The interviewer may also use the summary to make an overall competence rating.

STANDARDS

An essential element of the rating process is the matter of standards. Unless one has a rating scale which has been developed to provide built-in standards (e.g., behaviorally anchored rating scale), the interviewer will have to consider what standard he/she is using before beginning the rating process. If a scale with the anchors (lacks qualification, below average, average, above average, and highly competent) is used, the need for a standard is obvious. What is average? Is average a meaningful measure for employment purposes? The term average must be used in the proper context. In this approach average can be defined as average competence to perform the job. In this case competence is used in the legal sense. In legal terms competence means that a person has at least the minimum qualifications.

If the interviewer uses a five-point scale the highest level will be *highly competent*. In terms of competence, excellence is defined as efficiency. Definitions of competence already reviewed assume that the most effective performers do things differently than average performers. By trying to identify how the most effective people do things on the job and then to look for these characteristics in job applicants, the interviewer seeks to add a competitive edge to the organization by hiring people who are highly competent.

Taylor and O'Driscoll (1995) suggest that there are two possible rating standards. Applicants can be compared to the competences required by the job or they can be compared with other applicants. They prefer the former standard. They offer two reasons. First, comparing the applicant to required competences avoids the problem of offering a position to the best of the lot of applicants, all of whom fall short of minimum competence. Second, it is most desirable to evaluate applicants as soon as possible after the interview while the memory of the applicant is still fresh. By choosing a procedure of evaluating applicants against one another, the interviewer is making the assumption that ratings can be withheld until all applicants have been interviewed. This assumption is realistic only under certain circumstances (for example, when numerous interviews for the same position are conducted in the same time frame, or when interviews are tape-recorded for later evaluation). When applicants are rated against one another it is helpful to establish an objective scale. Taylor and O'Driscoll (1995) suggest the following: five equals top twenty percent of applicants; four equals sixty to eightieth percentile; three equals forty to sixtieth percentile; two equals twenty to fortieth percentile; one equals lowest twenty percent of applicants.

On any search for a new employee one should expect a full range of past performance behavior descriptions when all the applicants are considered. However, since many organizations only interview applicants who have been rigorously screened based on their resumés, there may be a restriction of range in the final applicant pool. Under these conditions one would expect to see a relatively high level of excellence and a low level of below-average competence in applicants interviewed.

A hypothesis testing model has been advanced by Rowe (1989). She states the following:

In any selection situation interviewers may test whether an applicant is a member of the target group of actual good applicants (i.e., a positive hypothesis test) or whether the applicant is outside the target group and so a potentially incompetent worker (i.e., a negative hypothesis test). In the first case, favorable information supports the hypothesis but is not conclusive as to whether the applicant is actually a good applicant, while unfavorable information, which indicates the applicant does not meet minimum standards for the job, proves the hypothesis false; that is, the applicant is a poor applicant and should be rejected. (86)

By setting up a standard for selection (the applicant is a member of the target group of actual good applicants) as a hypothesis, the interviewer is encouraging the use of positive information. This avoids the pitfall of overuse of negative information in the evaluation of applicants.

BEHAVIORALLY ANCHORED RATING SCALES

Considerable effort has been made to develop job related rating scales for performance appraisals. Some researchers are now suggesting that the same type of rating scales be developed for the employment interview. The anchors on the scale are geared toward factual aspects of the applicant's past. Such scales have anchors based on behaviors exhibited by ratees. In the case of an employment interview, behaviors exhibited by successful employees would be used to develop the anchors. It would be expected that interviewees would also have engaged in such behaviors in their previous experiences and that the interviewees would discuss those experiences during the interview. The ratings would be made based on the information provided by the interviewee. The behaviorally anchored rating scales are compatible with competence-based structured interviewing methods. An advantage of these scales is that they add a high degree of structure to the process of rating applicants. For example, the following scale on leadership is geared to the evaluation of extracurricular activities:

1 Acts independently
2. Member of club or activity
3. Long term member of club or activity
4. Founding member of club or activity
5. High officer of club or activity

When employee selection programs regularly process many applicants for the same position, such scales can be developed. Development of behaviorally anchored rating scales is a technical and time-consuming process. For specific details on how to develop behaviorally anchored rating scales, one should refer to a textbook on industrial and organizational psychology or HRM. In most instances, the more general type of scale suggested in this text (i.e., three- or five-point scales) will be the best choice for the interviewer.

THE EVALUATION RATING FORM

Most traditional approaches to the evaluation of interview data are based on the chronological patterns established in the interview, namely, work experience, educational background, interests, and activities. This approach is apt to be not as clearly job related as an approach based on employee competence. The evaluation rating form may be used to make ratings on applicants based on scales developed from competence factors. The anchors in a five-point scale are as follows: lacks qualifications, below average, average, above average, and highly competent. Whereas during the interview notes tend to be factual and descriptive of behavior, the notes made on the evaluation worksheet are a form of documentation. In general, the remarks summarizing a rating will be interpretive in character, although the interviewer will often wish to weave in supporting information of a factual nature. Either material from interview notes or interpretations of what an applicant said may be included as documentation of a rating.

After rating the applicant on each employee competence factor, the interviewer is ready to summarize his/her findings by listing the applicant's specific assets and liabilities. Most importantly, the summary should provide a condensed thumbnail sketch of the applicant, stated in terse, concise language. It should be stated in terms of assets (pluses) and liabilities (minuses). Conscientious completion of the evaluation rating form will also help organize the interviewer's thinking and will contribute to a more accurate appraisal. It will enable one to clarify ideas and will point up what one knows, and doesn't know, about the applicant.

CASE STUDY OF SALLY ARMSTRONG

To illustrate the use of the evaluation rating form the author returns to the assistant manager example that starts in Chapter 3. Rating scales based on the employee competence factors which were extracted from the job analysis and critical incident analysis have been developed. The data which was given by an applicant are used to make ratings. Following is a evaluation rating form filled out for the applicant Sally Armstrong, who was featured in the interview transcript in Chapter 4. The rating form is depicted in Figure 5.2. Ratings are made on the following four scales: (1) Work Experience; (2) Interpersonal Skills; (3) Educational Background; and (4) Career Interest. There is also a summary rating on overall competence. Documentation is provided for each rating.

RATING ERRORS

As one conducts interviews and evaluates the results, one must keep in mind some human frailties. Interviewers have biases which tend to influence any evaluative thinking in which the interviewer engages. Even the most egalitarian person needs to realize that rating errors are widespread. The most blatant form of bias is racial, ethnic, or sexual in nature. Since these forms of bias arc so important and are proscribed by law, Chapter 6 is devoted to them. The interviewer should be aware that overt bigotry is only one form of bias. Stereotypes are a more subtle form of bias, yet they can influence rating in a similar manner. While some stereotypes are harmless and others may be useful, stereotypes are a very dangerous aspect of employment interviewing in general. A reliance on stereotypes in selection may result in employment discrimination.

Among the typical rating errors in employment interviewing, the most common is the halo effect. This rating error occurs frequently in everyday life. If one rates a person high on one quality, one often tends to rate them high on other qualities. The high rating tends to influence a rater to give other high ratings as well. The halo effect works in reverse, also. A very negative rating on one quality may result in many negative ratings on other, nonrelated qualities. There is only one remedy for rating error: awareness. An awareness of the possible rating errors may prevent a rater from making them. It is something for every interviewer to work on.

Interviewing research has revealed a rating error called the contrast effect. Interviewers tend to rate Applicant B in relation to Applicant A. If Applicant A was superb, it makes it more difficult for Applicant B, who has just followed. Interviewers tend to rate Applicant B lower than Applicant A. The contrast effect seems to work against an applicant who is interviewed immediately after a very good applicant. The high qualifications of Applicant A overshadow Applicant B, even if Applicant B is well qualified. The way to guard against the contrast effect is to use a well-defined standard. When rating against a standard, the contrast effect is minimized.

Figure 5.2
Evaluation Rating Form

Instructions for Evaluation Rating Form

The first step is to fill in the name of each relevant competence factor. The ratings are made on five point scales. To complete the form simply place a check (✔) above the term which best describes the applicant's behavior.

Explain each rating you make. Try to be objective as you write your explanation. The best way to document a rating is to illustrate what the applicant said in the interview. Refer to Competence Evaluation Guides for examples of documentation.

After completing the rating scales, make a summary rating. The summary rating can be an average of all the scales or a weighted average, using the success factor codes as weights.

Evaluation Rating Scales

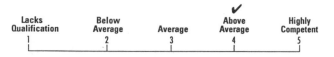

Lacks Qualification	Below Average	Average	Above Average	Highly Competent
1	2	3	4	5

Competence Factor: Work Experience

Applicant worked summers and part time while in school in a fashion retail store. Two years of full-time experience as a salesperson after college. Knows the stages in the sales process used by our store personnel. Consistently ranked highest among peers in previous jobs. Always met sales goals and was given a good work schedule as a result. Applicant has knowledge of cash handling procedures. Applicant did not explain the layaway procedure she claimed she used in a previous job. Has knowledge of ladies retail terminology. Is able to detail current fashion trends. Applicant has not had responsibility at assistant manager level in previous employment. She is familiar with all elements of store operations, but she has yet to prove herself in this capacity.

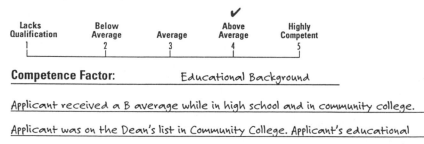

Lacks Qualification	Below Average	Average	Above Average	Highly Competent
1	2	3	4	5

Competence Factor: Educational Background

Applicant received a B average while in high school and in community college. Applicant was on the Dean's list in Community College. Applicant's educational program is relevant to the job opening.

Figure 5.2 (continued)

Lacks Qualification	Below Average	Average	Above Average ✔	Highly Competent
1	2	3	4	5

Competence Factor: Interpersonal Skills

Applicant expressed a desire to interact with both customers and fellow team members. Applicant stated that she is a team player and the interviewer assessment is in accord with the applicant's self-description. Good sense of how to maintain relationships in a store. Bouncy and talkative but appeared nervous during the interview. Interrupted the interviewer on several occasions. Seemed a little too anxious in terms of maintaining a conversation.

Lacks Qualification	Below Average	Average	Above Average	Highly Competent
1	2	3	4	5

Competence Factor: _____

_____

_____

_____

_____

_____

_____

Lacks Qualification	Below Average	Average	Above Average	Highly Competent
1	2	3	4	5

Competence Factor: _____

_____

_____

_____

_____

Figure 5.2 *(continued)*

Summary Rating

Candidate's Name: **Interviewer's Name:**

Sally Armstrong   Ann Jones

Overall Competence	Lacks Qualification 1	Below Average 2	Average 3	✔ Above Average 4	Highly Competent 5

Basis for Rating:

The applicant is knowledgeable about ladies fashion retailing. This knowledge is based on both her academic background (A.A. in Merchandising) and on actual experience in retail. The applicant has not had management experience. Her main strength is her outgoing personality and an aggressiveness which will aid in achieving high sales levels. This applicant would be ranked above average overall.

☒   **Average**
❏   **Weighted Average**
❏   **Other (explain)**

Summary Documentation:

Interviewers are often confused by the initial impressions error. There tends to be a rush to judgment at the beginning of the interview. This is because the initial impression one forms of the applicant is often so strong that one seeks to maintain it despite evidence which comes later. Interviewers are often accused of searching for negative information. Such a search may be motivated by a desire to uphold a negative initial impression. There is such a quality as first impact. A person with a strong first impact may be a valuable employee under certain conditions. The interviewer should not, however, let first impact influence his/her judgment or his/her conduct of an interview. The interviewer should follow the interview schedule whether or not the applicant makes a strong first impact.

Interviewers may succumb to the similarity effect. Interviewers tend to like and to respect people who are like themselves. If one is an interviewer and an applicant presents himself/herself as being like the interviewer, he/she should not favor them. Liking is not a basis for selection in an employment context.

TURNOVER RISK AND ADVANCEMENT POTENTIAL

One aim of a rigorous selection procedure is to avoid hiring people who will fail to adapt to the organization or job demands and drop out quickly. This is a challenging prediction to make. Another aim of selection is to hire people who have the potential to move ahead over time and achieve either technical superiority or higher levels of management. Again, this is a challenging prediction situation. The most difficult prediction to make is who will be the superior performers in jobs once they have been socialized into the organization, completed their first assignment, and made the commitment to advancement within the organization. In terms of a competence model, this means predicting who will develop into the most efficient performer on the job. Therefore, the essence of the evaluation process is to make a prediction about future performance. The interviewer expects that the applicant selected should not only be employed in the future but should be an above-average (at least) or (preferably) excellent employee.

During the hiring process, the interviewer should be aware of the issue of turnover risk. Turnover risk is defined in terms of a new hire who does not stay on the job long enough to justify the time and expense used to fill the position.

As in any other HRM function, experience and judgment play a key role in selection of new employees for an organization. While one may be able to develop a formula to predict who will turn over and who will advance, such formulae are useful only where there are large numbers of employees, large numbers of applicants, and stable organizational structures. In other cases the interviewer uses rules of thumb which may or may not work. At worst, a rule of thumb may stereotype applicants. For example, a large employer in the metropolitan region of a large city did a study that showed employees who lived in the suburbs turned over less than employees who lived in the city. The implication of the study was that the company should favor job applicants who lived in suburban locations. A rule of thumb may also work against an employer. What if a former teacher who is unemployed because of a reduction in force applies for a secretarial position? The teacher reasons that there are few openings for teachers and many openings for secretaries, so why not? The interviewer reasons that there is no way this person will stay with the job long term—the former teacher is considered to be overqualified and is not hired. While rules of thumb may be useful, the interviewer should try to keep an open mind on the issue of turnover risk.

Some applicants may clearly be disqualified because of previous incidence of job-hopping (e.g., four jobs in five years). Other applicants may be disqualified because they are overqualified. They appear willing to take a job way below their previous levels. Such employees may become dissatisfied in a short time and leave. Many applicants are seeking to start over in a new field and should not be disqualified because of age or lack of fit with the typical applicant profile. While it is not feasible to query directly about turnover risk, it is possible to infer the reasons why an applicant desires to perform a job. A typical procedure used by interviewers is the exploration of gaps in the applicant's school or work record. The interviewer should be sure to have a complete chronological record of the applicant's past activities. The interviewer should question each gap until he/she has a complete record; the material uncovered will help analyze turnover risk. Through this process of inference the interviewer can determine if there is sufficient evidence to conclude that the applicant will persevere and remain with the organization.

The importance of turnover risk varies. If a job entails considerable training then an employer will be very careful to select people who can successfully complete the training. Retaining people after training is completed is often dependent as much on organizational policies (i.e., compensation, career opportunities, and working conditions) as it is on the qualities of the employee. On the other hand, some organizations tolerate high levels of turnover among lower-level employees. It is believed that the most talented and motivated people will rise in the organization and remain. The others should move on. This idea is oftentimes sound in theory but unrealistic in practice. Often the best people leave (for more money or opportunity) and the mediocre employees hang on for the long term.

Turnover risk is one area where an interviewer's intuition can pay off. If one believes that an applicant is not being forthright in the interview, one's suspicion may be justified. That is why a separate rating scale for turnover risk is often a good idea. Documentation for a rating of high turnover risk could be concrete (e.g., job-hopping) or more qualitative (lacks career motivation). If the interviewer firmly believes that the applicant will cut and run once training or experience is received, then a high turnover risk rating is justified.

Another challenge to the interviewer is to predict advancement potential. Often the interviewer must make a judgment on this factor. In some organizations recruiting is conducted at the best schools and only the highest performing graduating students are accepted. These applicants clearly have a lot of potential. In other organizations there are fast-track or internship programs which are also geared to highly qualified applicants. One way of assessing advancement potential is to examine the cultural fit between the applicant and the organization. An organization has a corporate culture. Employees who adapt to the culture are more likely to remain than those who do not (this also applies to turnover risk). If one draws up a list of key aspects of the corporate culture which impact the open job, one can compare the applicant with these elements of corporate life. The interviewer should ask him/herself, Has the applicant shown anticipatory socialization to some of the cultural elements? The interviewer should ask him/herself if he/she thinks the applicant can and will adapt to the corporate culture.

Another aspect of advancement is the potential to enter management. Some issues to evaluate are, Has the applicant held leadership positions in the past? Is the applicant highly intelligent? Does the applicant have realistic career aspirations? Is the applicant high on achievement motivation or some other relevant motivation? Has the applicant made significant accomplishments in the past such as, in school, in the military, in previous jobs, in community or extracurricular activities, or in hobbies? An applicant with a strong pattern of past achievements of this type stands a good chance of advancing in most organizations.

EDUCATION, WORK EXPERIENCE, OUTSIDE ACTIVITIES

The evaluation procedure in the competence-based structured employment interview breaks down an applicant's background into basic elements, namely, employee competence factors. Evidence as to whether an applicant excels or is qualified on a particular employee competence factor may come from any aspect of a person's background or from behavioral intentions.

The interviewer may want to evaluate broad segments of an applicant's background if they are relevant job requirements. There are some basic considerations for evaluating educational background, which is often a job requirement. To evaluate high school education consider the following: type of course followed (academic or vocational), grades for each course taken, rank in class during each year of school, the academic quality of the school (SAT scores are useful here), academic honors, and recommendations. To evaluate college education consider the following: academic standing of the college, grades for each course taken, academic standing of the major department, academic honors, scholarships, how education was financed, rank in class during each year, and recommendations.

There are some basic considerations for evaluating the competence factor of work experience. Obtain a chronological history of work experience. For each job held obtain the job title, major duties and responsibilities, training received, promotions received, salary, accomplishments, reason for leaving, and total length of employment at the job. Ascertain if the applicant has been following a career path and obtain recommendations. Check out any gaps in the employment record to see reasons for them. To evaluate other aspects of an applicant's background consider extracurricular activities at school, sports, community activities, hobbies, and interests. Has the applicant shown creativity? Has the applicant made any outstanding accomplishments or contributions? Has the applicant demonstrated interpersonal skill, teamwork, and oral communications skill in these activities? How has participation in activities prepared the applicant for work?

COMPLEX DECISION MODELS

The final selection decision is a matter of judgment. Although the use of numerical formulae for the combination of rating scales into an overall score is not mandatory, it is sometimes advisable to transform ratings before reaching a final decision.

The most common transformation of ratings is called weighting. Some ratings are given more weight (two times or three times more) than others in reaching the overall rating in the summary. The basis for weighting should be the job analysis, job description, or some job-related information. In the competence model worksheet, the success factor code yielded the following ratings: one equals slightly important to job success; two equals moderately important to job success; and three equals extremely important to job success. As suggested in Chapter 3, these ratings could be the basis for assigning weights to employee competence factors.

In the retail store manager's job, for example, previous experience in retail management could be given extra weight, since there is no substitute for this.

Another process which is typical in employment interviewing is a compensatory model of evaluation. Strong points in an applicant's background can compensate for weak points. Many interviewers (and applicants) believe that a negative admission in an interview is fatal. While this may be the case, it is the interviewer's role to continue the discussion and downplay the negative information. Later, during evaluation, the interviewer can decide whether the negative admission is a knock-out factor. Typically, negative information yielded by applicants or lack of experience and qualifications may be viewed as minuses. Most applicants, despite efforts to present themselves in a positive light, will have some minuses. This is especially true when there are especially high standards for the job. A minus may be defined as a low rating on a scale, a lack of qualification and experience, a negative admission (a red flag) or a gap unexplained in the resumé or application. The minus is distinguished from the knock-out factor, which is the lack of a key requirement (a must) or which may be a character flaw (e.g., proven dishonesty). Unfortunately, many applicants will have minuses. The recommended procedure is to balance pluses and minuses. If the applicant has more pluses than minuses they may still be qualified for the job. For some positions (e.g., Supreme Court Justice) this approach cannot be used.

Often an applicant will be interviewed by several people as part of the selection process. In order to have a reliable final rating, it is desirable to develop a single rating for each competence factor and a single summary rating. This may involve coming up with a consensus set of ratings (combined ratings) based on discussion. Another possibility is the mathematical averaging of ratings to come up with one score which can be used to compare applicants. According to Conway, Jako, and Goodman (1995) the mechanical combination of ratings (i.e., averaging or summing) is preferred. They found no evidence that multiple ratings increased reliability when they were combined subjectively, but they caution that this is not a definitive finding. According to Taylor and O'Driscoll (1995), if there are several interviewers, each interviewer should make their individual ratings for each competence factor before combining their ratings. This procedure will help maintain objectivity.

A worksheet is helpful at this stage of the process. A sample worksheet is illustrated in Figure 5.3.

Taylor and O'Driscoll (1995) suggest that where large numbers of applicants are involved, a cutoff score can be developed for deciding who will be hired. All applicants achieving the cutoff score will get a job offer. In terms of competence, a practical cutoff is meets minimum competence level.

Very often the interview ratings and evaluation are not the only elements in the final selection decision. Where test scores are available, for example, it is often the case that interviewing is relegated to a secondary role. This may be appropriate if the tests are highly valid. A more balanced approach is often needed. Tests tend to be discriminatory and are often only marginally useful (i.e., low validity). In such cases test scores should be only part of the selection decision and should be balanced with other factors in a compensatory manner. In the final weighing of the applicant's assets and liabilities, one should try not to be unduly influenced by only one factor to the exclusion of other considerations. Weigh all of the evidence in an objective and impartial manner, aiming at a sound selection decision based on good common sense and valid facts.

It will be helpful for the interviewer to ask him/herself the following questions while evaluating an applicant's qualifications:

1. Consider *technical qualifications*—the extent to which the applicant is able to handle the particular job assignment. If there are deficiencies, consider whether training can make up for them.

2. Given that the applicant is able, consider whether he/she is willing to perform the job. All jobs are performed in a work context (working conditions) and environment (climate). Analyze whether the work aptitudes possessed by the applicant will promote successful completion of his/her initial and future assignments.

3. In particular consider whether the applicant possesses the interpersonal competence necessary to work with others. This is most important in people jobs and less important in technical work which is performed alone.

Figure 5.3
Evaluation Worksheet

Instructions for Evaluation Worksheet

When multiple interviews have been conducted with one applicant, the ratings of each interviewer can be combined to form a summary evaluation score. Ratings may be combined into a mathematical average or can be based on a discussion leading to a consensus decision. The worksheet can be used to facilitate this process. Summary evaluation scores are important if the interview process is to be validated at a later time. Compute scores for each competence factor and for overall competence.

Competence Factor	Interviewer Ratings			Summary Evaluation Score
	Interviewer A	Interviewer B	Interviewer C	

Basis for Score: ❏ Weighted average   ❏ Consensus discussion
                   ❏ Mathematical average   ❏ Other (describe)

APPENDIX 5.A
EVALUATION RATING FORM

Instructions for Evaluation Rating Form

The first step is to fill in the name of each relevant competence factor. The ratings are made on five point scales. To complete the form simply place a check (✔) above the term which best describes the applicant's behavior.

Explain each rating one makes. Try to be objective as you write an explanation. The best way to document a rating is to illustrate what the applicant said in the interview. Refer to Competence Evaluation Guides for examples of documentation.

After completing the rating scales, make a summary rating. The summary rating can be an average of all the scales or a weighted average, using the success factor codes as weights.

Evaluation Rating Scales

Lacks Qualification	Below Average	Average	Above Average	Highly Competent
1	2	3	4	5

Competence Factor: _____

Basis for Rating: _____

_____

_____

_____

_____

_____

_____

Lacks Qualification	Below Average	Average	Above Average	Highly Competent
1	2	3	4	5

Competence Factor: _____

Basis for Rating: _____

_____

_____

_____

_____

_____

Appendix 5.A *(continued)*

Lacks Qualification	Below Average	Average	Above Average	Highly Competent
1	2	3	4	5

Competence Factor: _____

Basis for Rating: _____

_____

_____

_____

_____

_____

Lacks Qualification	Below Average	Average	Above Average	Highly Competent
1	2	3	4	5

Competence Factor: _____

Basis for Rating: _____

_____

_____

_____

_____

_____

Lacks Qualification	Below Average	Average	Above Average	Highly Competent
1	2	3	4	5

Competence Factor: _____

Basis for Rating: _____

_____

_____

_____

_____

_____

Summary Rating

Candidate's Name: **Interviewer's Name:**

_____   _____

Overall Competence	Lacks Qualification	Below Average	Average	Above Average	Highly Competent
	1	2	3	4	5

Basis for Rating:

_____

_____

_____

_____

❏   **Average**
❏   **Weighted Average**
❏   **Other (explain)**

Summary Documentation:

_____

_____

_____

_____

_____

_____

_____

_____

APPENDIX 5.B
COMPETENCE EVALUATION AND DOCUMENTATION GUIDES

The following Competence Evaluation and Documentation Guides are provided to illustrate possible applicant responses to structured interview questions. First, the employee competence is provided. Then, possible applicant replies to questions are illustrated. A plus (+) before a possible answer indicates a favorable rating would result from this reply. A minus (–) before a possible answer indicates an unfavorable rating would result from this reply. The descriptive items which follow each competence factor may be used as models for the Basis for Ratings section of the Evaluation Rating Form (see Appendix 5.A). For a comprehensive set of possible applicant responses to interview questions, the reader should refer to Hakel (1970). The author acknowledges Hellervik (1977) who developed the method of documenting applicant responses illustrated in this section.

COMPETENCE EVALUATION
AND DOCUMENTATION GUIDES

Employee Competence: Achievement Motivation

A desire to excel or succeed in competitive situations as evidenced by taking responsibility and taking calculated risks to achieve goals.

Documentation of Applicant Qualifications

+   The applicant completed school in a timely manner.
–   The applicant seems to always look for the easiest way to do something.
+   The applicant set challenging goals.
+   The applicant welcomed increased responsibility.
+   The applicant has been recognized for achievements.
+   The applicant has been involved in continuing education.
+   The applicant has become conditioned to hard work and long hours.

Employee Competence: Adaptability

The ability to make changes in one's self or one's behavior in order to deal with changing circumstances, changing living conditions, and changing levels in organizational hierarchy.

Documentation of Applicant Qualifications

+   The applicant changes an objective when it is no longer appropriate.
+   The applicant has changed a plan in order to adapt to changing conditions.

- Rationalization is used to explain differences between closely held beliefs and actual behavior.
- Pragmatism outweighs ideals or values most of the time.

Employee Competence: Attention to Detail

Perception of key aspects of a situation. Taking details into consideration during the planning process.

Documentation of Applicant Qualifications

+ The applicant double-checks work before releasing it in order to avoid errors.
+ Attention to detail has led to successful performance in a project.
- The applicant's only concern is for the big picture.
- The applicant expects staff people to attend to the details.

Employee Competence: Efficiency

Having and using the requisite skills, knowledge, and ability. Concern for effective performance.

Documentation of Applicant Qualifications

+ The applicant has the skills required for the open position.
+ The applicant has the knowledge required for the open position.
+ The applicant has a record of accomplishment.
- The applicant does not reach milestones in a timely manner.
- The applicant is not able to maximize the resources of a budget.

Employee Competence: Interpersonal Skill

Managing interactions in a work setting in a pleasant and effective manner. The ability to relate to coworkers at various levels, including higher and lower levels.

Documentation of Applicant Qualifications

+ The applicant enjoys being a part of group situations.
- The applicant appears strongly motivated to be number one in a group, taking more credit than he/she may actually deserve.
+ The applicant spends his/her free time involved in group activities.
+ The applicant performed successfully in group activities on the job.
+ The applicant displays good listening skills.
- The applicant tends to work on solo projects and jobs.

+ The applicant displayed an ability to reduce conflict, such as, smoothing out problems between coworkers or helping others.
− There have been problems with supervisors or teachers that reflect a tendency to lose control.

Employee Competence: Leadership

Able to develop a sense of the mission of the organization or group and take action to influence others to work toward accomplishment of the mission.

Documentation of Applicant Qualifications

− The applicant shows a tendency to let others dominate.
+ The applicant's personality has charisma.
+ The applicant appears willing to stand up for what he/she believes is right.
+ The applicant has been an officer of a club or organization.
+ The applicant has been a military officer.
+ The applicant has successfully motivated groups of people.
− The applicant does not know how to motivate others.
+ When placed in an authoritative position, the applicant is effective.
+ The applicant has been successful when coordinating a group effort.
− The applicant has not displayed initiative.

Employee Competence: Mental Ability

Intelligence level of an individual as measured by verbal ability, mathematical ability, the capacity to reason logically, and the ability to learn in organizational settings.

Documentation of Applicant Qualifications

+ The applicant is able to respond in detail to abstract questions.
− The applicant's educational decisions and work have often been unsuccessful.
+ The applicant has caught on quickly to new assignments at work or school.
+ The applicant is able to understand complex questions.
− The applicant's hard work generally is not reflected in his/her grades.
+ The applicant uses an extensive vocabulary.

Employee Competence: Oral Communication Skills

The ability to speak clearly. The ability to use language in an interesting and informative manner to communicate information within an organization. The ability to lead meetings or to participate in meetings.

Documentation of Applicant Qualifications

+ The applicant can listen effectively.
+ The applicant chooses words appropriately.
+ One can clearly understand what the applicant says.
− The applicant is vocally inexpressive or monotonic.
− There a tendency for the applicant to ramble.
+ The applicant asks meaningful and appropriate questions.
− The applicant's nonverbal behavior is annoying or strange.
+ The applicant is able to articulate his or her points in an interesting way.
− The applicant exhibits poor usage of the English language.

Employee Competence: Organizational Commitment

Desire to remain with organization despite ups and downs of day-to-day problems, and a likelihood of maintaining a long tenure in an organization.

Documentation of Applicant Qualifications

− The applicant speaks about past employers in a negative manner.
− The applicant has a history of poor attendance or tardiness.
+ The applicant put in extra effort to attain goal accomplishment in the past.
− The applicant shows signs of being a job-hopper.
− The applicant gives excuses for leaving jobs which appear unjustified.
+ The applicant has shown a tendency to stay with a job despite difficulties.
+ The applicant adjusted well to schools and work life.
+ The applicant returned to the same part-time jobs on school breaks.

Employee Competence: Planning and Organizing Ability

Setting goals for accomplishment of objectives. Developing a course of action in order to accomplish goals within an established time frame. Structuring activities in order to maximize effectiveness of one's time.

Documentation of Applicant Qualifications

− The applicant spends too much time in unplanned activity.
− There is evidence to support the view that he/she takes on more projects than he/she can finish.
− The applicant often gets to the end of a time period without accomplishing his/her original objectives.
+ The applicant effectively and appropriately planned work assignments.

+ The applicant has followed a clear career path.
+ The applicant took a methodical approach to past assignments.
+ The applicant seems to do high priority tasks first.
+ The applicant continues working on a task until completed, despite disruptions.

Employee Competence: Stress Tolerance

The ability to work under conditions of high pressure, competition, adversity, and maintain a high level of performance.

Documentation of Applicant Qualifications

− He/she tended to carry on about job dissatisfactions (or quietly brood) without making an attempt to remedy the situation.
+ He/she seems to accept responsibility for problems or mistakes that actually were of his/her own doing.
− The applicant exhibited a tendency to rationalize failures or disappointments.
+ He/she has shown evidence of withstanding peer pressure or persisting in an un-popular cause to a realistic extent.
+ The applicant has ways of reducing job-related stress.
− The applicant appears nervous or tense.
+ The applicant accepts constructive criticism and uses it to his/her benefit.
− The applicant reported losing his/her temper frequently when under pressure.

Employee Competence: Technical Ability

Able to utilize the core technologies of a job in order to produce expected results.

Documentation of Applicant Qualifications

+ The applicant has past achievements in the field.
− He/she has performed poorly in courses relevant to this field.
+ The applicant gives concise and accurate answers to technical knowledge questions.
+ The applicant has had part-time jobs in this or a related area.
− The applicant admits to not feeling confident in his or her background of this area.
+ The applicant has a history of past successes in the area.
+ The applicant has taken courses in the relevant area.
+ He/she has earned exceptional grades in job-related courses.
− The applicant is unable to discuss any particular accomplishment relevant to the technical area under consideration.

+   The applicant demonstrates an interest in the technology through some previous involvement.
+   The applicant has favorable recommendations which refer specifically to mastery of the technology.

Employee Competence: Turnover Risk

Previous behavior indicates that the applicant may not remain employed long enough to make a meaningful contribution to the employer.

Documentation of Applicant Qualifications

+   Applicant has an employment history without significant gaps.
−   Applicant has a history of job-hopping.
+   Applicant is capable of moving up in the organization.
−   Applicant has indicated that he/she has previously been terminated from employment for just cause.

Part III

Equal Employment Opportunity Issues

Chapter Six

Equal Employment Opportunity and the Employment Interview

The methods proposed in this book are consistent with equal employment opportunity (EEO) laws, regulations, and court decisions in the U.S. Employment procedures are highly regulated at this time. It is important to note that these regulations have been sustained over thirty years, though many political shifts have occurred during that time. However, the reader is encouraged to keep current on changes in regulations and to adjust employment procedures accordingly. Also, the reader is advised to obtain state regulations pertaining to employment interviewing which are in force at the present time.

If the interviewer follows the suggestions contained in this book, not only will his/her organization benefit from sound HRM selection practices, but it will be protected from law suits arising from charges of employment discrimination brought by applicants.

In order to have a complete picture about EEO, the reader should possess some knowledge on the following topics: job analysis, predictive validity, content validity, job relatedness, consistency (reliability, standardization), and work experience requirements. On the other hand, this book does not cover some issues which are also quite important to EEO. Some of the EEO hiring-related issues not emphasized in the book are the following: recruiting, employment testing, preemployment medical examinations, reference checking, sexual harassment, and background investigations. The reader can obtain information on these issues from texts on HRM.

HISTORICAL PERSPECTIVE

Dipboye, Arvey, and Terpstra (1976) provide a legal framework for the question, Are employment interviews discriminatory? Their emphasis is on the concept of adverse impact. They state that for the employer intent on maintaining fair employment practices, the first question to answer concerns whether the company's hiring procedures result in disproportionate rejection of women, blacks, and other protected groups included under Title VII of the Civil Rights Act of 1964 (a result which is termed *adverse impact*). The Civil Rights Act of 1991 upheld the use of statistical methods for determining evidence of adverse impact. The interview is one potential source of adverse impact. If the interview results in adverse impact, *then* it must be validated. Court decisions have clearly established that subjective hiring practices that have a discriminatory impact are subject to court action under the Civil Rights Act of 1964. A valid selection procedure may be used, despite problems of adverse impact, if its use is considered to be a business necessity.

The structured interview methods described in this book constitute an objective basis of employment interviewing which could withstand a challenge of employment discrimination if validated.

Dipboye, Arvey, and Terpstra (1976) point out that one major implication of EEO laws for employment interviewing is that there are now restrictions on preemployment inquiries. Any question which has an adverse impact on a group protected by Title VII of the Civil Rights Act of 1964 is prohibited unless such inquiry has been demonstrated to provide information relevant to whether a person can perform a job successfully. Guidelines set forth by state human rights commissions as to what inquiries can be made are often more explicit than Federal guidelines.

The New Jersey Division on Civil Rights has published rules and regulations on preemployment inquiries. Some examples from this regulation will illustrate the level of detail which an interviewer must master. With regard to a person's name, it is discriminatory to inquire about the fact of a change of name or the original name of an applicant whose name has been changed. With regard to birthplace and residence of an applicant, it is discriminatory to inquire about the birthplace of an applicant, the birthplace of an applicant's parents or evidence of the applicant's birth certificate, naturalization, or baptismal record. With regard to creed, it is discriminatory to inquire about private organizational affiliations of an applicant or political affiliations of an applicant. With regard to age, it is discriminatory to inquire about the age or date of birth of an applicant (except when such information is needed to fulfill legal regulations). With regard to national origin and ancestry, it is discriminatory to inquire about an applicant's lineage, ancestry, national origin, descent, parentage, or nationality. Likewise it is discriminatory to inquire about the nationality of the applicant's parents or spouse. With regard to language, it is discriminatory to inquire about the applicant's mother tongue, the language commonly used by the applicant or in the applicant's home, or how the applicant acquired the ability to read, write, or speak a foreign language. With regard to organizational affiliations, it is discriminatory to inquire about all clubs, social fraternities, societies, lodges, or organizations to which the applicant belongs, other than professional, trade, or service organizations.

The following sections deal with the legal framework as it applies to employment.

The Equal Pay Act of 1963

This law prohibits employers from paying employees of one sex less than employees of the opposite sex "for equal work on jobs the performance of which requires equal skill, effort, and responsibility, and which are performed under similar working conditions . . . ." This law is intended to guarantee women the same pay for performing work which is substantially similar or identical to work performed by men. Substantially similar jobs can have different job duties and job names and still be considered legally equivalent jobs.

Title VII of the Civil Rights Act of 1964

This law bans all discrimination in employment because of race, color, religion, sex, or national origin. It covers most aspects of employment practice, and it holds the employer responsible for any discrimination that goes on within the employer's organization. Reporting requirements designate the following races as being of specific concern: Blacks, Asian Americans, American Indians, and Spanish-surnamed Americans. However, all races, including Whites, are protected by Title VII. The Equal Employment Opportunity Commission (EEOC) is charged with enforcing Title VII. Originally the EEOC could only investigate charges of discrimination, but a 1972 amendment to Title VII gave the EEOC the right to initiate civil law suits. If the EEOC determines upon investigation that there is reasonable cause for the complaint, its first step is to resolve the issue through conciliation. If conciliation efforts fail to resolve the problem satisfactorily, suit may be brought.

The EEOC handles large class action suits involving broad patterns of discrimination as well as smaller individual suits. Some of the charges which have led to law suits are as follows:

- Unvalidated tests for hiring and promotion resulting in adverse impact
- Using unlawful hiring criteria adversely affecting women and minorities, such as, arrest records, height, weight, or family status
- Imposing a high school diploma requirement without showing job relatedness
- Discrimination in recruiting, testing, hiring, training, job assignment, pay, hours, transfer, and promotion
- Excluding blacks from supervisory, clerical, sales, skilled, and technical jobs
- Excluding female employees from supervisory positions and certain shift assignments
- Using more stringent promotion criteria for women than men

As a part of its investigative function, the EEOC has issued a series of guidelines and policy statements which guide employers in the conduct of sound business practice. Among these documents are the following: *Guide-*

lines on Sex Discrimination, Guidelines on Religious Discrimination, Guidelines on National Original Discrimination, Guidelines on Employee Selection Procedures, and *Policy on Pre-employment Inquiries.* A body of case law is being built up around Title VII, and these cases must be considered in interpreting this law. For example, the Supreme Court has held that the *Guidelines on Employee Selection Procedures,* while not law itself, must be given "great deference" by the courts in judicial process. These guidelines deal with the use of tests in the selection process, but the term test is broadly defined to include both scored and unscored employment interviews as well as ability tests which are designed to measure eligibility for transfer, promotion, training and for retention. Also, specific qualifying or disqualifying personal background items are considered tests. These include personal history, educational history, work history, biographical information blanks, and application forms. Various states also have laws and regulations regarding employment discrimination.

An important concept highlighted by legal proceedings pursuant to the Civil Rights Act is that discrimination can be defined in terms of both disparate impact and disparate treatment. *Disparate impact* refers to statistical evidence of discrimination. In trial proceedings related to cases of employment discrimination, courts have accepted evidence of discrimination, such as, unequal pass–fail rates of actual applicants for jobs, statistical evidence comparing the race/sex/ethnic percentage of the general population in a particular geographical area with the race/sex/ethnic percentage of the employer's workforce, and significant differences between protected groups as they are distributed throughout the levels of the employer's organization or compared to how they are distributed in other similar organizations. In *disparate treatment* cases, plaintiffs must establish either directly or inferentially that they were intentionally treated less favorably than similarly situated majority group members. This requires that the plaintiffs establish that the employer's motivation was discriminatory in nature (Arvey and Faley, 1988).

The Age Discrimination Act of 1967

This act, which covers the same employees as Title VII, bans discrimination because of age against anyone at least forty years old but less than seventy.

Americans with Disabilities Act of 1992

Title I of the Americans with Disabilities Act (ADA) prohibits employment discrimination on the basis of disability. The ADA protects a qualified individual with a disability from discrimination in job application procedures, hiring, advancement, discharge, compensation, job training, and other terms, conditions, and privileges of employment. To be protected a person must be a qualified individual with a disability as defined by the ADA and implementing regulations. With regard to an individual, the term *disability* means a physical or mental impairment that substantially limits one or more of the major life activities of such individual. A physical or mental impairment means any physiological disorder, or condition, cosmetic disfigurement, or anatomical loss affecting one or more of the following body systems: neurological, musculoskeletal, special sense organs, respiratory, speech organs, cardiovascular, reproductive, digestive, urinary, genital, lymphatic, skin, endocrine, or any mental or psychological disorder, such as, mental retardation, organic brain syndrome, emotional or mental illness, and specific learning disabilities. In many cases it is obvious that a condition is an impairment. In other cases it is not obvious. When it is not clear that a job applicant has an impairment, the interviewer can ask for medical documentation that describes the condition which the applicant has in his/her possession. For more detailed information regarding what to do in the case of a specific disability, refer to the relevant EEOC Compliance Manual.

In October 1995 the EEOC released final enforcement guidance on preemployment disability-related questions and medical examinations. Under ADA, employers cannot ask job applicants disability-related questions or conduct medical examinations until they have extended a conditional job offer. This is to help insure that an applicant's possible hidden disability (including a prior history of a disability) is not considered before the employer evaluates an applicant's nonmedical qualifications. Employers can only inquire about an applicant's ability to perform specific job tasks and nonmedical qualifications at the pre-offer stage. Once a conditional offer has been made, the employer may ask disability-related questions and require medical examinations as long as this is done for all entering employees in that job category. If the inquiry or medical examination screens out an individual because of a disability, the employer must demonstrate that the reason for the rejection is job related and consistent with business necessity.

EEOC Guidelines for Employee Selection (1978)

These guidelines are a complex legal document which are designed to provide a basis for developing acceptable employment tests and for evaluating a company's testing and employee selection procedures. The assumption of the guidelines is that a well-conducted selection program can be beneficial to both company and employees, but that a poorly conducted program may be perpetuating discrimination in a needless manner. The employment interview is covered by this regulation.

The key to understanding the guidelines is a knowledge of the process by which a selection procedure is developed and validated. According to the guidelines a business may utilize a selection procedure having an adverse impact on a minority group, providing that the procedure has great utility, that its use is deemed a business necessity, and that there are no acceptable substitutes to the use of the procedure. Validation may be accomplished in the following three ways: (1) *Content validity* implies that the procedure consists of suitable samples of the essential knowledge, skills, or behaviors composing the job in question; (2) *Construct validity* shows that the procedure statistically relates to known psychological concepts; and (3) *Predictive validity* is a demonstration of the procedure's effectiveness in selecting employees whose future job performance will be above average.

THE RELEVANCE OF THE
LAW TO EMPLOYMENT INTERVIEWING

The EEOC Guidelines on Employee Selection Procedures squarely address the role of employment interviewing not only in hiring but also in transfer and promotion transactions. They stipulate that the basis for questioning an applicant or employee should be factually related to the job opening under consideration. Given that a question is job related, it must also be able to be applied with consistency to all minority groups and females. Any question which works against one these classes may be considered to be discriminatory unless it has been validated against successful job performance and it has been found to be a matter of business necessity.

Two other important concepts are the four-fifths rule and the bottom-line concept. The four-fifths rule states that the acceptance rate for minority job applicants should be at least four-fifths (eighty percent) of the acceptance rate for nonminority job applicants. The acceptance rate is also known by its technical term, *selection ratio*. The selection ratio is the number of applicants selected divided by the total number of applicants. If there are 100 applicants and twenty-five are hired, then the selection ratio is 1:4. The four-fifths rule is based on comparing selection ratios for minority and nonminority applicants. In the example, if there are 100 nonminority applicants and twenty-five are hired, and if there are 100 minority applicants, then at least twenty must be hired in order to comply with the four-fifths rule. If this ratio is not obtained, there is a case for statistical evidence of employment discrimination (adverse impact). A major problem with employment tests is that minority applicants may score well below nonminority applicants. If the test were the sole selection procedure, the four-fifths rule would be violated in these cases. Often employers have dropped the use of employment tests in order to remove the possibility of statistical discrimination resulting from overzealous use of employment tests. However, the four-fifths rule applies to all selection procedures. All employers should be mindful of this rule and check periodically to see if their interview procedures or other selection procedures are responsible for inordinate rejection of minority applicants.

For a long period of time some employers sought to get around the four-fifths rule by using different test norms for minority and nonminority applicants. In practice minority applicants could get hired with lower test scores than nonminority applicants. This practice was justified by calling it affirmative action. However, using two different standards based on the same selection procedure also leads to charges of reverse discrimination. The Civil Rights Act of 1991 made the use of dual standards illegal. While dual standards are less likely to be a problem in employment interviewing, the interviewer should be aware of this pitfall.

Another statistical aspect of employment discrimination is the bottom-line rule. The bottom-line rule was established because of the inevitability that some selection procedures will be discriminatory. An employer can continue the use of the discriminatory procedure without penalty if it can show that the procedure does not result in fewer minority group members being hired at the bottom line. In other words the employer must take affirmative action to see to it that the discriminatory procedure is offset by other selection procedures (e.g., employment interviews) in order to produce comparable selection ratios for minority and nonminority applicants.

Another relevant issue is termed bona fide occupational characteristics (BFOQ). This legal term refers to the rare situation where there is a business necessity to discriminate among job applicants. Airlines have been successful in imposing age restrictions on pilots. Police and fire departments have been successful in imposing strength tests on their members. Many other occupational requirements have been shown to be based on stereotypes rather than business necessity and have been discontinued.

STEREOTYPES

While some stereotypes may have some basis in fact, it is more likely that they are an oversimplification of the truth. Be especially sure to go beyond using stereotypes which unduly categorize minorities and females by getting the actual facts about such job applicants. Stereotyping is a common practice in business organizations and other large organizations. Stereotyping undoubtedly leads to problems in the selection of employees. Arvey (1979) reviewed seventeen studies which, when summarized, showed that females were generally given lower evaluations than males when these candidates had similar or identical qualifications. Such stereotyping is even more evident for certain types of jobs. Research findings showed that older persons and handicapped persons also tend to receive lower interview evaluation ratings than people who are not in these categories. Such bias may not be completely attributable to stereotyping as there are numerous other factors (e.g., rating errors) which lead to biased evaluations. Organizations should systematically review all HRM ratings (e.g., selection, performance review) to ascertain that race, gender, age, or handicap are not leading to lower ratings.

Interviewers must avoid direct or indirect statements that may exhibit hiring preferences for males or females, unmarried or married people, childless women, or women with children. Statements, such as, We've always had single women in this job, may come back to haunt interviewers. Also, avoid references to any beliefs that the interviewer or others in the company might hold about women or minorities or what work is proper for women to do. It is extremely difficult for interviewers to separate their own personal values from what they look for in others, but imposing personal values on others in a work situation may be both inappropriate and illegal.

Similarly, one should avoid making comments that allude to stereotyped views of women or minorities as groups. References to such matters as emotionalism in women, aggression (or passivity) in minorities, or a male dislike for women supervisors are undoubtedly not true of all members of that group and are therefore inappropriate. While it may be true that some men, for example, may not want to work for a woman, it is certainly not true that all men would not work for a woman.

What essentially happens in any employment interview is a process of communication. The interviewer obtains information and impressions from which to predict the future performance of the applicant in the position that is vacant. Because of the difficulty in predicting complex performance from a brief interview, it is clear that shortcuts in the selection process can lead to problems. These shortcuts frequently involve the use of stereotypes to classify people. Of course, as stereotypes they may not accurately reflect the actual credentials of the candidate. Some of the following commonplace stereotypes may affect employment interviews and the evaluation of applicants:

- A well dressed person is probably successful.
- An older person is not adaptable.
- A younger person is not yet experienced enough to handle major responsibility.
- An applicant who's been out of work too long is not an attractive candidate.
- Applicants who have not had good salary growth do not produce results in their work.
- A person who communicates well is probably effective on the job.

No one is completely free of predetermined attitudes and values. There is probably some identification with stereotypes in virtually every evaluation made in an interview. It is important as an interviewer to be aware that these attitudes are simply shortcuts and not necessarily the truth. Conclusions based on stereotypes should be cross-checked with other information and periodically checked against actual performance to see if they are correct.

RACIAL AND RELIGIOUS DISCRIMINATION

Racial discrimination has figured in many prominent court decisions involving employment. The penalties have been large. Not only racial discrimination but also discrimination based on religion is strictly prohibited. The following lines of inquiry should be avoided:

1. Religious affiliation, including church, parish, or religious holidays observed by the applicant
2. Applicant's race or color of skin, eyes, hair, and so forth
3. Photographs with application or at any time before hiring
4. Information about a person's family, family history, or parents' occupations

NATIONAL ORIGIN

Some interview inquiries are inadvisable because they may be construed to be inquiries about national origin, such as the following:

1. Asking about a name change or the original name, if changed
2. Birthplace of applicant and applicant's parents
3. Inquiries about lineage, ancestry, national origin, descent, parentage, or nationality of applicant, parent, or spouse
4. Applicant's mother tongue, language commonly used by applicant at home, or how the applicant acquired the ability to read, write, or speak a foreign language
5. Name and address of any relatives of the applicant

An interviewer may ask if the applicant is a citizen of the United States and, if not, whether or not he or she has a working visa and permission to remain permanently in the United States in order to conform to immigration requirements.

EDUCATIONAL STANDARDS

Asking whether a candidate has a high school diploma or college degree is not in itself discriminatory if the job really requires such educational qualifications. The Supreme Court, however, explicitly affirmed EEOC guidelines that prohibit requiring a high school education as a condition of employment when the requirement disqualifies minorities at a substantially higher rate than others and when there is no evidence that it is a significant predictor of job performance. This means that requirements for a high school diploma or college degree should be eliminated if these qualifications are not needed for the job in question.

REALISTIC EXPERIENCE REQUIREMENTS

Experience requirements should be reviewed and reevaluated to assure that they are necessary for particular jobs. The same is true for skill requirements that may be screening out minority or female candidates. These requirements often affect these groups, who, because of past discrimination, have not been able to gain the required experience and skills.

ARRESTS AND CONVICTIONS

Arrests and convictions fall within the realm of EEO interviewing because of several technicalities which must be observed. Most important is the fact that an arrest record must have no bearing in an employment decision. It is best not to inquire about whether or not a person has been arrested.

Convictions, however, do bear on employment decisions. An employer may refuse employment to a person who has been convicted of a crime. In making such a decision it is important to consider the severity of the crime, the relevance of the crime to the job opening, and how long ago the incident occurred.

AGE

Age is important both in the employment interview and in situations where promotions are concerned. The EEOC is as concerned with promotions as it is with initial selection, and the promotion process should be objective. While it is necessary to bring young people up to higher levels, it is also important to consider candidates for a job opening on the basis of merit. For this reason any interviews relating to promotion (or transfer) should be granted to all applicants, unless there is a job-related exception.

COMMUTING

It is not advisable to ask an applicant how he/she will get to work. The location of the job and available commuting arrangements can be detailed, however. This gives the applicant the information he/she needs to make a determination about whether or not he/she could get to work promptly and regularly. It is then up to the applicant to determine whether he/she can make the commute on a regular basis.

MILITARY EXPERIENCE

Questions about military experience or training are permitted but there are several off limits areas here. Inquiries may not be made about the type of discharge received. Since minorities tend to receive fewer honorable discharges than nonminorities, there is a danger of discriminatory stereotyping.

Further restrictions include not asking about eligibility for military service, whereabouts in 1914–19, 1941–45, 1951–53, and date of discharge. An interviewer may not ask about military experience in non-U.S. forces.

DIFFERENTIAL BEHAVIOR OF INTERVIEWEES

Arvey and Faley (1988) point out that minority applicants may behave in a manner that is unfamiliar to interviewers. They cite research which indicates that white interviewers may misread black applicants who "emit verbal and nonverbal behavior that is acceptable or even desirable in their subculture, but this same behavior may be misinterpreted or confused by a white interviewer" (222). It is also possible that women, older workers, and handicapped individuals also differ in their reactions while taking interviews which could contribute to lower evaluations. For example, older candidates may be more thoughtful and cautious in their interview responses than younger candidates, according to Arvey and Faley. Many candidates for business positions today suffer from a relative lack of experience or coaching from family and friends on the nature of the business world and effective conduct during an interview. If the candidate seems defensive, hostile, passive, or aggressive could these reactions be wholly or partly attributable to nervousness? Do not expect everyone to appear nervous, but if the candidate is nervous, recognize the fact and try to make him or her more comfortable.

BENDING OVER BACKWARDS

When confronted with new and unfamiliar constraints in interviewing and hiring, the tendency of some people has been to bend over backwards in order to conform to EEO regulations. This practice is not only poor business judgment but could get the company into trouble in another way. Reverse discrimination may be defined as ruling out applicants in favor of less-qualified applicants who are members of minority groups. Choose the applicant best qualified for the job on the basis of merit. It is not at all necessary to hire an applicant on the basis of minority status alone.

CURRENT EQUAL OPPORTUNITY ISSUES

An article by Campion and Arvey (1989) summarizes research issues relating to equal opportunity and the employment interview. Despite the potential for lawsuits stemming from interviews, there have been few such suits. Campion and Arvey reviewed 8,000 employment discrimination lawsuits which occurred between 1979–87 and found that an employment interview figured in seventy-two of them. The three major types of discrimination provoking the seventy-two lawsuits were gender (forty-seven percent), race (thirty-one percent), and age (twelve percent). These statistics indicate that despite bias on the part of some interviewers, the employment interview is not on the endangered list of HRM procedures likely to become extinct.

Campion and Arvey (1989) point out that recent research has shown that fears of pervasive interviewer bias are unfounded. It is the uninformed interviewer who is most likely to be biased. As interviewers are provided with more information about applicant competence or job requirements and as they make more use of the structured interview, their tendencies to rate in a biased manner are diminished. Bias only occurs in certain situations. For example, some interviewers have no bias against women for one type of position but show bias when another type of position is involved.

Employment interviewing represents a grey area in the application of the uniform guidelines. The employment interview is considered to be a subjective procedure from a legal standpoint. Subjective procedures are held to a different standard than objective procedures (such as tests). A subjective procedure is considered discriminatory if it results in disparate treatment between applicants. In other words, all applicants should be treated in the same manner. A statistical standard for determining discrimination is not required for this type of selection procedure, and discrimination is judged on a case-by-case basis. If there is discrimination in a particular case, the entire organization is not held to be guilty of discrimination.

There are several components to establishing the selection process as being nondiscriminatory. They are the following:

• Job relatedness (based on a job analysis)
• Standardized (same procedure for all applicants)
• Uses questions which do not result in information and ratings based on affected class membership

Campion and Arvey (1989) point out some problem areas in employment interviewing at this time. They are pre-interview deterrence (recruitment), selection and training of interviewers, and subjectivity in evaluation. The risks in the recruitment area are the following:

• Not advertising openings
• Using word-of-mouth advertising
• Giving preference to relatives and friends
• Discouraging applicants
• Use of unnecessary job-experience requirements

There have been some court decisions critical of organizations which have no interviewers who are members of minority groups or protected classes. A more frequent criticism has been the lack of adequate or current training for employment interviewers. The courts have been critical of employment interviewing procedures which result in highly subjective evaluations. One way of removing subjectivity is to make the process job related. Another way to reduce subjectivity is to provide interviewers with guidelines on how to rate interviewees. Of course, validation of the employment interview process reduces subjectivity. Another way to reduce subjectivity is to introduce a review process. Things to be reviewed are question strategy, evaluation standards, and interviewer recommendations. A review of employment interviewing can be a part of the regular HRM procedures audit which occurs in many organizations.

Arvey and Faley (1988) review a number of research findings about discriminatory effects of the interview. Studies have been conducted using equally qualified minority and nonminority applicants and measure whether minorities receive lower evaluations than nonminorities. They find that, in general, differential evaluations as a function of applicant sex are likely in interview situations and that they are not confined only to male interviewers. Also, the type of job interacts with gender to influence the evaluations given. "The contextual situation is an important factor in evaluating the likelihood of bias in the employment interview" (231). For example, when females apply for jobs that are considered traditional male jobs, they receive lower evaluations. Similarly, males applying for stereotypically female-type jobs also receive lower evaluations compared to females. It is well established that the physical attractiveness of the applicant may bias interviewer evaluations. The gender of the subordinates who will work for a job candidate, if hired, has been shown to influence interview results. In one study, female candidates were evaluated more favorably when the subordinate was also female. Likewise, male candidates were given high evaluations when their potential subordinate work force was also male. In terms of race, research indicates a tilt in favor of blacks. According to Arvey and Faley, one possible factor that accounts for higher evaluations given to black candidates is that interviewers may have been sensitive to EEO and affirmative action issues and legal issues. The results of research on age indicates a fairly pervasive bias against older job candidates in the employment interview.

Part IV

Review of the Literature on Employment Interviews

Chapter Seven

Highlights from Previous Reviews of the Literature

A section on research on employment interviewing must acknowledge the contributions of researchers over a long period of time. While research findings from the 1960s may seem dated, they are significant for several reasons. They highlight that our current state of the art has been made possible by steady and patient research conducted over a long period of time. Also, they show that what is being recommended today as a way to improve the competence level of work organizations is based on revelations made many years ago. There is always a lag between personnel research findings and changes in business practices. In the case of employment interviewing, this lag has been particularly long.

Periodically, a scholar will review the literature on employment interviewing. These reviews provide a picture of the state of the art in this procedure. They also provide some practical information for the managers who seek to improve their skills in employee selection. Some reviews of the employment interviewing literature include Mayfield (1964), Dipboye, Arvey, and Terpstra (1976), Schmidt (1976), Arvey and Campion (1982), Webster (1982), and Harris (1989).

Some of the major findings of Mayfield's (1964) review were the following:

- General suitability ratings based on unstructured interviews have low reliability.
- Material is not covered consistently in unstructured interviews.
- Interviewers are likely to weight the same information differently.
- Structured interviews result in higher interrater reliability.
- Interview validity is low.

- If the interviewer has valid test information, his/her predictions based on the interview plus test information are usually no better and frequently less valid than the predictions based on the test alone.
- Interviewers can reliably and validly assess intelligence but have not been shown to be effective in evaluating other traits.
- The form of the question effects the answers given.
- The attitude of the interviewer effects the interpretation of interviewees' responses.
- In unstructured interviews, interviewers tend to talk most.
- Interviewers are influenced more by unfavorable than favorable information.
- Interviewers make their decisions quite early in unstructured interviews.

While Mayfield wrote a landmark review of the literature, a common bias against the employment interview underlies some of his conclusions. Cronshaw and Weisner (1989) have called this bias the "doctrine of interview invalidity." This refers to the theme, promulgated by many researchers, that the interview is not as effective a predictor of future outcomes (e.g., turnover, advancement) as tests. Furthermore, the interview is more expensive to administer than an employment test. Researchers suggest that the interview represents an inefficiency which ought to be reduced (or eliminated).

Schmidt's (1976) review was the first to catalog the information processing bias sources that limit interviewer accuracy. Some of the conclusions reached by Schmidt in his literature review are as follows:

- Interviewers often reach a final decision early in the interview, typically within the first four minutes. This finding is controversial and is not universally accepted, however.
- Interviewers weigh negative information more heavily than positive information. This is the unfavorable information effect, first identified by Springbett in 1958. This finding has generated much subsequent research and is still controversial.
- Early impressions are more important than factual information in determining interviewers' judgments.
- After interviewers form a favorable impression, they spend more time talking than the interviewee.
- Interviewers possess stereotypes of idealized successful applicants against which real applicants are judged.

Dipboye, Arvey, and Terpstra (1976) pointed out the following problems with regard to the validity of the employment interview:

- Interviewer judgments are less reliable than objective tests. Reliability in this instance refers to the agreement among different interviewers regarding the same candidate. A frequent finding in personnel research is that professional interviewers seldom attain a level of consistency among themselves in their judgments that would ensure accurate predictions of job success.

- Interviewers display the human characteristic of forgetting information provided in the course of interviews. A typical rationalization is to forget those items that contradict one's final decision.
- Interviewers tend to give insufficient weight to favorable information on job candidates. In many cases the employment interview becomes a search for negative evidence.
- Judgments by interviewers are too often based on superficial characteristics that are unrelated to subsequent job success, such as, physical characteristics, manner of dress, race, or sex.

Arvey and Campion (1982) highlighted the following issues in their review:

- Board or panel interviews increase reliability and validity of the process.
- Use of job analysis to form questions increases the reliability and validity of the interview process.
- Rating errors (e.g., primacy–recency effect, first impressions, and contrast effect) are common in the interview.
- Only thirty-three percent of interviewers make decisions during the first half of the interview.
- Research on bias in the interview clearly highlights that race, gender, and handicaps of applicants influence interview decisions.
- Verbal behavior is more important than nonverbal behavior in the interview.

Webster (1982) wrote an influential review summarizing two decades of work on employment interviewing. The research summarized in this volume focuses on a microanalytic approach which highlights factors influencing interviewer judgments. Among the contributions of this research, according to Dipboye (1992), is a cataloging of cognitive biases committed by interviewers, including, stereotyping, overweighting of negative information, snap decisions, primacy effects, and contrast effects.

Dipboye (1992) wrote a review of the literature on employment interviewing which focused on process perspectives. He states the following:

The striking aspect of post-interview judgments is the extent to which they are dominated by global impressions of the applicant's qualifications with little attention to variations among different dimensions of the applicant's qualifications . . . . A large part of the variance in post-interview judgments of qualifications is attributable to a general performance factor, reflecting the tendency of interviewers to be particularly impressed with applicants who are fluent, responsive, and somewhat assertive in their behavior and who have a good physical appearance . . . . Interviewers appear to form global impressions of an applicant's suitability on how they come across in the interview, and these broad, highly subjective factors appear to influence final evaluations more than the objective credentials of the applicant. (119)

Interviewers appear to be influenced by the applicant's paper credentials, the comments of other interviewers, and the first impression made by the applicant.

This applies not only to post-interview judgments but also to the conduct of the interview itself. This finding reflects Hakel's (1982) earlier conclusion that "It is abundantly clear that whatever information occurs first has a disproportionate influence on the outcome of interviews" (136). Furthermore, interviewers who have favorable attitudes towards an applicant tend to show more signs of approval and fewer signs of disapproval in their verbal and nonverbal behavior during an interview. Dipboye (1989) summarizes by stating that "confirmatory biases can prevent post-interview impressions from contributing to the prediction of the criterion in at least two ways. These biases could prevent the interviewer from generating and retaining new information. Once their initial impressions are fulfilled, interviewers seem less likely to seek additional, unique information which might improve on the prediction obtained from pre-interview impressions alone" (57–58).

The highlights from previous reviews illustrate that there is still a lot of ambiguity in research on the employment interview. Some of the findings of Arvey and Campion (1982) are contradictory to findings made by previous investigators. These findings may be due to improved methodology, research design, or insight. It is more likely, however, that discrepant research findings are due to the fact that the complexity of the employment interview process defies current research designs. Eder and Ferris (1989) provide the following overview, which is useful in interpreting the results of literature reviews: "Recent literature reviews have suggested that low interview validity is likely the result of both passive and active judgment errors made by interviewers as they gather, retrieve, and process applicant information" (11). Further clarification is provided by Eder, Kacmar, and Ferris (1989). They state the following:

Unlike other selection techniques, standardization in the analysis of applicant qualifications is made more difficult by the informal extemporaneous style of most interviewers, and by the interviewer's limited ability to extract veracity from applicant self-reports of alleged competence. Clearly, the inherent information processing limitations and non-job relevant biases of the interviewer disadvantage the interview in comparison with more standardized selection decision tools. (18)

It may not be possible to understand the microprocesses of interviewing at this time due to methodological limitations. Another problem is that research on employment interviewing does not take place in most organizations which make extensive use of employment interviews. Many managers have confidence that their selection procedures are valid and do not see the need for research. Compared to the enormous number of employment interviews which are conducted, the current level of research is miniscule.

A major problem with interview research is that many researchers conclude that the employment interview is redundant and an unnecessary part of the selection process. It is abundantly clear that business organizations consider the interview an essential part of the selection process. Researchers claim that other parts of the process (i.e., application form, resumé, and tests) are more reliable sources of information about the applicant. Why, they argue, use less reliable methods when better (and cheaper) methods are available? Sometimes cost or efficiency are not sufficient to determine a business practice. The employment interview has that face-to-face characteristic which is an essential part of an employment decision for many organizations. Therefore, the goal should be to improve the interview process.

Chapter Eight

Panel Interviews

The panel interview is growing in popularity. It is a natural outgrowth of the desire for more structure in the employment interview. The panel interview may not be appropriate in some organization cultures, may be impractical due to scheduling requirements or geographical factors, and may be viewed as an unwelcome change by some. However, the benefits of this method are becoming better known. This chapter will explore some issues related to the panel interview.

BACKGROUND ON PANEL INTERVIEWING

In many public-sector organizations, the panel (or board) interview is commonplace. In some cases this form of interview is mandated by labor contracts or the organization's rules and regulations governing employee selection. The fundamental principle behind the panel interview is that it assures the interviewee's responses to questions will be heard uniformly by each interviewer.

The panel interview is by definition a structured interview. While there are many variations possible, this methodology lends itself to structure. The questions posed to applicants for a position are invariably the same from applicant to applicant. This is less easy to control when there are multiple one-on-one interviews. Other aspects of the interview which are uniform in panels are the length of the interview, the way people are chosen to be in the panel, the setting of the interview, and the method by which evaluation of applicants is conducted. There is a lot of standardization (consistency) which can be brought to bear on the selection process if panel interviews are used.

While there is a high emphasis on interviewer skill in a one-on-one interview, the emphasis is on standardized administration of the interview in the panel. In the one-on-one interview, the interviewer is often concerned with presenting an organizational image. This can interfere with good communication because the interviewer may be selling rather than analyzing the applicant's strengths and weaknesses. In the panel interview, the emphasis is on making sure all the questions are asked and that the applicant has adequate chance to respond. In the panel interview, the interviewer has a better chance to take notes since the task of interview administration is shared. The panel interview is thought to be fair by applicants, and the image of the hiring organization may be enhanced if it is used.

COMPARISON BETWEEN PANEL INTERVIEWS AND THE ASSESSMENT CENTER METHOD

It is interesting to compare and contrast the panel interview with the assessment center method. In the assessment center method, candidates are observed by assessors in role plays and simulations. Once the candidate has performed, the assessors commence to make ratings. Typically a candidate is rated on five to fifteen dimensions which have been ascertained to be job related. Ratings are made based on behavior exhibited during the role plays and simulations. During the meeting when ratings are made, the procedure is to discuss each candidate's performance and to make a single rating for each dimension. The rating represents a consensus among the assessors present at the meeting. A summary rating is also made for each assessee. The summary rating indicates the assessors' opinion of the overall management potential of the assessee. This summary rating is also made by consensus. There is a parallel between the assessment center method and the panel interview procedure. The panel also generates ratings on specific factors and an overall rating. The panel decides by consensus as do assessors in the assessment center method.

The panel interview generates behavioral information about the applicant. This information is likely to be quite rich in detail. It is likely to be related to the competence factors to be rated, since the questions were developed to yield information on these factors. The panel members will have a meaningful discussion of the applicant's interview data before making ratings. In a decision-making process based on consensus, there is a tendency for extreme views to be moderated or thrown out. In the process of arriving at a consensus, each rater gets to contribute his/her unique perspective and perception of the applicant. The multiple opinions are a valuable input into the final selection decision, and in some cases, the panel's ratings determine the final hiring decision.

If the panel seeks to arrive at a consensus on each competence factor and on a summary rating, this evaluation process will parallel that used in an assessment center. It should be added that assessment center ratings have shown high predictive validity for selection purposes. A HRM professional has suggested that the structured interview would be a low-cost alternative to assessment centers (Lowery, 1994).

THE PANEL INTERVIEW TECHNIQUE

The panel interview technique is featured among the standard interview techniques advocated by several HRM professionals. Dipboye (1992) reviews the literature on group interviews. Campion and his colleagues (Campion, Pursell, and Brown, 1991) feature panels in their structured interview procedure. Latham and his colleagues (Latham, Saari, Pursell, and Campion, 1980) advocate a panel interview in his situational interviewing approach. Bell (1992) advocates panels in his "structured interviewing" approach. Warmke and Weston (1992) present practical information on how to implement panel interviews in corporate settings.

Dipboye (1992) cites a *Forbes* article ("Surviving the Group Interview," March 24, 1986, 190–191) which estimates that group interviews constitute twenty percent of all interviews. He goes on to cite three aspects of group interviews which enhance the validity of the employment interview. "First, a group of interviewers should recall material from the interview better than an individual interviewer. Second, the aggregation of interviewer opinions, whether in the form of simple averaging or consensus decision, should improve the quality of decisions by correcting and balancing out random error. Third, the diverse information and opinions that multiple interviewers bring to the task of judging the applicant can enhance accuracy of judgment" (210).

Campion, Pursell, and Brown (1991) suggest that having an interview panel reduces the impact of idiosyncratic biases that single interviewers might introduce. They recommend that the panel should consist of a subset of experts who helped analyze the job and develop the interview questions. This is recommended because of the experts' familiarity with the job and questions. They recommend at least three panel members, including supervisors of the job to be filled and a HRM representative. They recommend using the same panel members for all interviews to increase consistency. They suggest that the panel should be assembled well in advance of the first interview to review job duties and requirements, questions and answers, and the interview process. They suggest that panel members should not review application forms, resumés, or other materials prior to the interview. This may cause the panel to form impressions that could bias their subsequent evaluations of the candidates. They suggest that all panel members record and rate the candidates' answers during the actual interview.

This recording should be exactly as the candidate responded. If that is not possible, special care should be taken to provide clear paraphrases and abbreviations. These recorded answers become a critical part of the documentation. Candidate responses must be able to be reconstructed accurately in case a particular hiring decision or the entire process is ever challenged. All candidates are asked the same questions. There is no prompting or follow-up questioning because this decreases standardization of the interview. Questions may be repeated if necessary. (254–255)

They suggest that all panel members should be present before the candidate enters the room.

One selected member of the panel asks all the questions for all the candidates to ensure consistency. Between successive candidates, the panel members should not discuss the questions, the answers, or the candidates in order to avoid potential bias from changing standards or comparisons among candidates. After all the interviews are completed for a given job, any large discrepancies between interviewers are discussed. Candidates are allowed to ask questions in a subsequent non-evaluation interview with a (human resource management) representative. (255)

Bell's (1992) recommendations for panel interviewing closely parallel those of Campion, Pursell, and Brown (1991).

Latham, Saari, Pursell, and Campion (1980) propose a situational interview which is based on asking behavior intention questions to job applicants. The applicant reacts to the question in terms of what he/she would do in a specified work-related situation. The applicant's response is evaluated based on a predetermined rating procedure. Critical incidents used to formulate questions are also used to determine behavioral anchors for the interview rating scales. The interview is administered in a panel format. There are three members of the panel. One panel member asks the situational questions. The other two panel members record the answers. There are no probe questions. The applicant is informed before the interview that the question will be repeated upon request. The applicants are not rated by the interviewers. The interview ratings are done by supervisory personnel who had been trained in rating procedures. The names of the applicants are not revealed to the raters to assure objectivity. The raters work in pairs. Each answer is scored independently and then through discussion one rating is agreed upon. Both the independent ratings and the consensus ratings are recorded. This procedure is like a test in its objectivity and is likely to yield highly reliable ratings. This method has also proven to be valid in terms of predictive validity.

Taylor and O'Driscoll (1995) suggest that if two or three interviewers conduct the interview, the roles of the participants should be clarified. One interviewer should be assigned to take notes. One interviewer should handle the opening and closing of the interview. There should be a prior arrangement about who asks which questions. Each interviewer should ask the same question in interviews with the various candidates, in order to assure consistency.

Warmke and Weston (1992) advocate the panel interview as a replacement of the one-on-one interview in corporate business settings. They cite Philip Morris and Virginia Natural Gas as two companies which have adopted this technique. Both organizations encountered initial resistance to the panel interview, so new adopters of the technique should anticipate that a change agent or change methodology will be needed to replace the traditional interview. This would be especially so if the panel makes the final hiring decision.

The companies adopting panel interviews cited the following reasons for their adoption: (1) a desire to improve the validity and accuracy of their traditional interview procedures; (2) reduce the costs and time of using an assessment center (or regular hiring procedures); (3) increase the consistency and defensibility of the selection procedures used within the company; and (4) foster a high level of buy-in or acceptance of selection and promotion decisions by both members of management and job candidates.

Warmke and Weston (1992) suggest that the selection of panel members be done with care because it can have a major effect on the outcome of the selection process. If an organization is beginning the implementation of the panel interview process, it is suggested that a HRM professional be included on the panel to avert probiems with EEO issues. It is always a good approach to include the new hire's future supervisor on the panel as well as higher-up executives. However, the inclusion of the future manager and higher-up executives poses the problem that they may have undue influence on the deliberations of the panel. Other members of the panel could be managers from departments with which the new hire will interact and technical experts (if the open position requires a moderate to high level of technical knowledge).

Warmke and Weston (1992) suggest that the questions to be used in the interview should be developed or at least approved by the members of the panel. Of course, all questions must be job related.

Warmke and Weston (1992) state that the content of the panel interviews used at Philip Morris and Virginia Natural Gas have the following format. The interviews begin with ice breakers and the introduction of panel members. The opening is usually followed by questions about experience, such as, "Can you begin by providing us a brief, chronological description of your education and work experience? What are your current job responsibilities? Which of your present or past job duties did you like most and why? What are your feelings about working overtime and swing shifts?" (121). The experience questions are followed by a series of questions intended to evaluate essential skills relevant to the job in question. This component of the Warmke and Weston model closely resembles the competence-based structured interview process recommended. Warmke and Weston suggest that the following additional types of interview questions may also be used: hypothetical questions, role plays to be performed by the applicant, and technical questions.

Warmke and Weston (1992) suggest that fifteen to twenty nontechnical questions can be asked in an hour. Brief technical questions that have predetermined responses usually take one to two minutes each. They suggest a desirable length for a panel interview is fifty to seventy minutes.

Warmke and Weston (1992) suggest the need for interviewer training is less in a panel interview format than in the one-on-one format. This is because the preparation for the interview is often done by HRM representatives. However, people conducting a panel interview for the first time need to be oriented

4. Develop a scoring guide for interviewers. This is not a scoring key, as intended behaviors will vary and there is not necessarily one right answer.
5. Conduct a pilot study to eliminate questions which do not yield a sufficient range of answers (i.e., low, medium, and high ratings) or which are difficult to score.

Taylor and O'Driscoll (1995) point out that a strength of situational interviews is their focus on tapping meaningful samples of behavior. Situations featured in questions should mirror events which actually occur on the job. They also emphasize that the situational interview is valid only to the extent that the employer follows all the steps in the process. There have been reports (Latham and Saari, 1984) of situational interview programs which have not led to high predictive validity coefficients because interviewers did not adhere correctly to situational interview procedures. In this case, interviewers did not record applicant responses to questions and then made ratings based on the same global impressions typical of the traditional interview. Taylor and O'Driscoll point out that the situational interview lends itself to being administered by a panel. Some of the pros and cons of the situational interview according to Taylor and O'Driscoll are the following:

- The high degree of structure reduces interviewer error due to varying abilities of interviewers.
- The degree of interrater reliability of interviewer ratings is increased.
- Validities of .40 have been achieved with this technique.
- The situational interview is accepted by both interviewers and applicants alike. However, since most applications of this technique have been for lower-level positions, the approach may not be suitable for some higher-level positions.
- The amount of preparation for this type of interview is great. It is usually undertaken by sophisticated HRM professionals. A consultant can be enlisted to assist in this process.

BEHAVIOR DESCRIPTION INTERVIEW

Janz (1989) quotes Lord Byron, who said, "The best prophet of the future is the past," in 1823. Janz observed that most interviews were conducted by means of the traditional method which focused mainly on applicant opinions and generalities as opposed to what applicants had actually done in the past. The patterned behavior description interview (PBDI) developed by Janz focuses on what applicants have accomplished (or did not accomplish), how they did what they did, and what was the context of their activities. Janz points out that there are four key types of interview information namely, qualifications (i.e., credentials), the applicant's prepared version of his or her previous experience, applicants' opinions (i.e., self-perceptions and behavior intentions), and behavior descriptions—detailed accounts of actual events from applicants' job and life experiences. The PBDI approach is based on the premise that behavior descriptions are the best way to predict future behavior based on past behavior. "Behavior descriptions reveal specific choices applicants have made in the past, and the circumstances surrounding these choices. The interviewer probes the details of the situation and what the applicant did in that situation, or what the applicant did the next time that same situation arose. Only then can the interviewer independently judge how well the applicant performed in that situation" (159).

The PBDI approach seeks to avoid the type of information generated in the typical employment interview. Therefore, credentials, experience descriptions, and opinions are not considered useful interview data (such data are collected elsewhere). What the interviewer seeks are behavior descriptions. Therefore, a picture of the applicant's behavior patterns is drawn. The more recent and the more longstanding the applicant's behavior patterns, the more likely the patterns will predict behavior in the future.

The behavior description interview concept has been developed into a practical employment procedure. For example, Motowidlo, et al., (1992) report a structured interviewing technique that they call the structured behavioral interview. Borrowing from Latham's and Janz' approach, the technique includes the following characteristics:

- It is based on the results of a critical incident job analysis.
- The critical incidents are analyzed and behavioral dimensions are derived from them.
- Questions are developed about how the candidate has handled past situations similar in nature to those which will be encountered on the job.
- Probe questions are an integral part of the interviewing process. They may be asked at the discretion of the interviewer. Probes seek details of the situation, what the candidate did, and what happened.
- The interviewer takes notes on the candidate's responses to questions.
- In the evaluation phase, the interviewer makes ratings on scales with behavioral anchors.
- The ratings are combined into an unweighted sum to yield a total interview score.

Motowidlo, et al., (1992) present research studies which show the validity of the structured behavioral interview. The development of the structured behavioral interview in a consortium of telecommunications companies is documented. The structured behavioral interview showed both moderate predictive and moderate concurrent validity in the selection of entry level management and marketing personnel. The "best single estimate of the criterion related validity of the structured behavioral interview, .22, is the empirically observed, uncorrected estimate, averaged over three studies with a total sample of approximately 500 interviewees" (583). The researchers found that their results were comparable to those found by other investigators in studies of the structured interview.

The Motowidlo, et al., (1992) study touches on several interesting interviewing techniques. It was found that both audiotaped and in-person interviews yielded similar results. Job performance was moderately predicted from audiotaped interviews where nonverbal cues were not available. The researchers explained that prediction was based on behavioral information and not appearances. A key finding was that people with strong interviewing skills elicit more behavioral information from candidates, which is crucial to the structured interview format.

Taylor and O'Driscoll (1995) note that an old adage of industrial–organizational psychology is an underlying principle of the behavioral description interview. The adage is that "past behavior is the best predictor of future behavior." According to Taylor and O'Driscoll:

Developing a (behavioral description interview) involves first conducting a job analysis, through which performance competences . . . are identified. Next, interview questions are developed which seek behavioral descriptions from job candidates for each competency. Behavioral descriptions are stories of actual situations applicants faced, how they responded (that is, their behavior) and the outcome to the situation. During the interview, candidates are asked both pre-prepared and follow-up questions to ensure that candidates provide complete behavioral descriptions, and the interviewer takes notes of these during the interview for later rating. Finally, candidates are rated on the quality and quantity of relevant behavior descriptions, and a final selection decision is made. (19)

Taylor and O'Driscoll state that the behavior description interview has become popular because it is relatively easy to develop, does not require a special scoring procedure, and can be used for jobs that have had few (or no) previous incumbents.

According to Taylor and O'Driscoll (1995), preparation for the behavior description interview is extensive. Also, the behavior description interview takes at least one hour to administer. Those who attempt to do a shorter version will not obtain sufficient behavior descriptions to make meaningful ratings. The behavior description interview is less effective for people with little work experience and those who have been out of the workforce for some time. These individuals will have relatively little recent experience to describe to the interviewer.

HIGHLY STRUCTURED INTERVIEWING TECHNIQUE

Campion, Pursell, and Brown (1988) propose a highly structured employment interviewing technique. The procedure is done in the following five steps:

• Develop questions based on a job analysis
• Ask the same questions of each candidate (no prompting or follow-up questions are permitted; repeating questions is permitted)

- Rating scales for scoring answers are anchored with examples and illustrations.
- An interview panel records and rates answers.
- The process is administered in a consistent manner to all candidates. Special attention is given to job relatedness, fairness, and documentation in accordance with testing guidelines.

This technique is similar to Latham (1989), but it utilizes other question types in addition to situational questions. Also included are job knowledge, work requirements, job sample, and simulation questions. Also, there are frequently questions on a candidate's background (e.g., experience, education) or willingness (e.g., shift work, travel). The latter types of questions may serve as warm up questions at the beginning of the interview.

In a well-known case study, referred to in Chapter 1, Campion and Arvey (1989) demonstrated the effectiveness of the highly structured employment interviewing technique. The interview developed using this technique had the following statistical characteristics: interrater reliability, predictive validity, test fairness for minorities and females, and cost-benefit utility.

Campion, Campion, and Hudson (1994) conducted a study to assess whether a structured interview can have incremental validity in the prediction of job performance above and beyond a battery of cognitive ability tests, and to test whether future-oriented (e.g., situational) or past-oriented (e.g., behavior description) questions have higher validity. Of interest in this study are the attributes of workers in a pulp mill identified by job analysis. These attributes are similar to employee competences. Some of the attributes were initiative, teamwork, resolving conflict, commitment to improvement, work ethic, safety orientation, accepting responsibility, growth orientation, and leadership.

Also of interest are examples of structured interview questions used in the Campion, Campion, and Hudson (1994) approach (note: both questions are intended to assess conflict resolution and collaborative problem solving knowledge, skills, and other requirements). The following is a future-oriented question: Suppose you had an idea for a change in work procedure to enhance quality, but there was a problem in that some members of your work team were against any kind of change; what would you do in this situation? Answers to the question are rated as follows:

Five equals excellent answer (top third of candidates). Explain the change and try to show the benefits. Discuss it openly in a meeting.

Three equals good answer (middle third). Ask them why they are against the change; try to convince them.

One equals marginal answer (bottom third). Tell the supervisor.

The following is a past oriented question: What is the biggest difference of opinion you ever had with a coworker? How did it get resolved? Answers to the question are rated as follows:

Five equals excellent answer (top third of candidates). We looked into the situation, found the problem, and resolved the difference. We had an honest conversation with the person.

Three equals good answer (middle third). Compromised; resolved the problem by taking turns, or I explained the problem (my side) carefully.

One equals marginal answer (bottom third). I got mad and told the coworker off, or we got the supervisor to resolve the problem, or I never had differences with anyone.

The highly structured employment interviewing technique (Campion, Pursell, and Brown, 1988) was used as the selection procedure. Uncorrected validities were .50 for the interview and .46 for the test battery. The interview has substantial correlations with the tests, but it still had incremental validity in predicting performance. Past questions had higher validity than future questions (but not significantly higher).

Pulakos and Schmitt (1995) performed a study using the same hypothesis as Campion, Campion, and Hudson (1994) about situational versus experience-based interview questions. They instituted rigorous controls to deal with methodological limitations of the Campion study. They found that only the experience-based interview showed a significant relationship with performance.

CONCLUSION

It is clear that there is no one best way to conduct a structured interview. In fact, a highly structured interview may not yield increased validity commensurate with the effort needed to conduct the interview process. However, it is also clear that some structure is better than none at all. The best advice at this point is to choose the structured interview method which is most in conformity to the needs and the capabilities of the hiring organization.

Chapter Ten

Validity of the Employment Interview

While this topic is inevitably technical, it is also essential. All organizations want to avoid discrimination charges and lawsuits. Having validated employment procedures is one way of doing so. The EEOC Selection Guidelines mandate that any selection procedure having a discriminatory effect must be validated according to job-related factors. They state that "the use of any selection procedure which has an adverse impact on the hiring, promotion, or other employment or membership opportunities of members of any race, sex, or ethnic group will be considered to be discriminatory and inconsistent with these guidelines, unless the procedure has been validated in accordance with these guidelines, or the provisions of Section 6 below (i.e., use of alternative selection procedures to eliminate adverse impact) are satisfied" (EEOC, 1978). The guidelines spell out in considerable detail how such validation studies should be conducted, and the reader is urged to obtain a copy of this document. In this chapter, two validation practices recommended in the guidelines are covered, namely, content validity and criterion related validity.

The research evidence on the usefulness of structured interviews also hinges on validity studies. Some of the most important studies are reviewed in this chapter.

CONTENT VALIDITY

Content validity in selection means that the selection procedure is designed to measure skills, knowledge, and abilities needed to perform a job. Content validation refers to the adequacy of a selection procedure in sampling the relevant and critical behaviors, knowledge, and skills necessary for job performance.

The adequacy of a selection procedure depends greatly on how well the items in the procedure directly reflect observed behaviors, skills, and knowledge considered essential, critical, or important for adequate job performance (Arvey and Faley, 1988). In theory, if the applicant performs well on a test of job-related items, that person can perform well on the job. The employment interview format suggested by this text provides adequate levels of content validity. The most basic element in establishing content validity is the job analysis. The job analysis reveals the key tasks, skills, knowledge, and abilities necessary to perform the job. These elements are often summarized in a job description. The process suggested in this text as a means of preparing for the interview assures that interview questions are job related. The standardization implied by the suggested interview schedules will assure that applicants receive only job-related questions.

According to Arvey and Faley (1988), the courts have increasingly acknowledged that content validity is an equally acceptable strategy in and of itself and not just a poor second choice to predictive validity. They state that since content validity has received more positive recognition from the courts as well as the developers of the various sets of selection guidelines, and because it is perceived by many to be less susceptible to the problems that plague the other validation categories (e.g., small sample sizes, restriction in range) it has been touted as a panacea for the various ills that surround validation. They state that it appears that evidence of a selection procedure's validity based on the content validity strategy can survive court review if the content validity study is reasonably well conducted and carefully documented.

Arvey and Faley (1988) cite the results of court cases which have hinged on a content validation approach. The following recommendations for content validity have been gleaned from these cases:

- A content valid test must contain all the critical job components as revealed by a job analysis. It is not enough to perform a job analysis. The selection procedure must reflect the important components revealed by the job analysis.
- The knowledge, skills, and abilities figuring in a selection procedure must coincide with some of the knowledge, skills, and abilities required to perform the job successfully.
- The attributes selected for examination must be critical and not merely peripherally related to job performance.
- The various portions of the selection procedure must be accurately weighted to reflect the relative performance to the job of the attributes for which it tests.
- The level of difficulty of the selection procedure must match the level of difficulty for the job.
- The primary emphasis in content validity is on the validity of the methods used in creating the selection procedure.
- The cornerstone in the construction of a content valid selection procedure is the job analysis or position analysis.

- The qualifications of subject matter experts who assist in the development of selection procedures is also important. The documentation of the development of content valid selection procedures is considered to be important.

- Legal and professional guidelines note that content validity is an inappropriate strategy for demonstrating the validity of selection procedures that purport to measure traits or constructs (e.g., intelligence, insight, judgment, and interests). The more closely the content of the selection procedure approximates tasks to be performed on the job, the more appropriate is the content approach for validation purposes.

Arvey and Faley (1988) detail the required steps for developing a selection procedure based on content validity. Job analysis is the first step. Then, test items or work samples (i.e., interview questions) that reflect tasks, behaviors, skills, knowledge, or abilities are developed. Experts who are familiar with the job (e.g., supervisors or job incumbents) are asked to evaluate the items of the selection procedure to determine if they are an accurate reflection of the job. The SMEs should also be able to identify items that are irrelevant to the job in question.

CRITERION RELATED VALIDITY

Another form of validity is called criterion related validity (predictive validity). In the case of employment interviewing, it involves the ability to obtain a statistical relationship between interview ratings and subsequent job performance. Job performance is measured in terms of salary increases, promotions, or supervisory ratings on objective aspects of performance.

Harris (1989) has written a review of the literature on employment interviewing. He provides a summary of recent validity studies (through meta-analysis) which shows that the employment interview has moderate predictive validity. Overall validity for all types of interviews is .29 uncorrected and .41 corrected for range restriction. For structured interviews, the validity is .32 uncorrected and .45 corrected for range restriction. An illustrative study was conducted by Campion, Pursell, and Brown (1988). A comprehensive structured interview consisting of four types of questions (i.e., situational, job knowledge, job simulation, and worker requirements) was administered. A highly structured scoring guide was used. Reliability was high ($r = .72–.88$). The validity coefficient for this approach was .34. The authors conclude that structured interviews can achieve useful validity. Some additional conclusions of the Harris review are as follows:

- Structured interview formats produce relatively high validity coefficients.
- Selective use of interviewers could lead to greater predictive accuracy.
- There is much recent evidence that applicant gender has little or no effect on interview ratings.

A recent review of employment interview validity was written by Cronshaw and Weisner (1989). They point out that the result of early research on employment interviewing was a "doctrine of interview invalidity." It was unfashionable to challenge this doctrine for many years, and many researchers may have been discouraged from rigorously studying interview validity. Until recently, most research was centered on microbased, social, psychological factors. Each of these studies points to one (or a few) aspects of the interview, which, if improved, will lead to more effective selection. The assumption of these studies has been that the interview is largely subjective. This subjectivity is seen as leading to errors and, therefore, invalidity. If interviewers improve their technique through study and mastery of the microprocesses, subjectivity will be less damaging to validity. This approach has not proven to be practical, since in order to improve the overall validity of the employment interview, each and every interviewer would have to strive to improve their technique. Many interviewers will not or cannot make such an effort.

Cronshaw and Weisner (1989) have adopted a point of view that by introducing structure to the interview process, validity will be improved. According to Cronshaw and Weisner, the main issues in employment interview research today are criterion related validity, economic utility, and bias in interview ratings. The approach used by Cronshaw and Weisner is called *meta-analysis*. This methodology operates by combining the results of all existing validity studies and gaining an overview. Also, statistical anomalies in previous research are factored in so a corrected validity coefficient can be obtained. In their study, Cronshaw and Weisner grouped all previous research studies into the following four categories: (1) structured interviews, (2) unstructured interviews, (3) individual (one-on-one) interviews, and (4) board (panel) interviews. The figures in a meta-analysis table express via correlational scale the strength of the relation between employment interview ratings (the predictor) taken at t_0 and job performance ratings (criterion) taken at t_1 (Nevo and Berman, 1994). Table 10.1 depicts Cronshaw and Weisner's results.

Two problems with the typical validity study are sampling error (a random sample is not available) and range restriction (only the best qualified applicants are interviewed). The corrected validity coefficients are a result of a statistical formula which shows what could be expected in a carefully controlled study. According to Cronshaw and Weisner's (1989) results, the employment interview is clearly a statistically valid predictor of future job performance. Adding structure to the typical job interview will improve its predictive capability. Also, it was found that the validity of the structured interview was highest when interview questions were based on a formal job analysis.

A meta-analysis of thirteen studies of structured interviews was conducted by Wright, Lichtenfels, and Pursell (1989). The study focuses on structured interviews only. The following four types of questions were included in the interviews studied: (1) situational questions, in which an applicant is asked

Table 10.1
Results of Meta-Analysis

Type of Interview	Number of Subjects	Mean Validity Coefficient	
		Corrected	Uncorrected
All studies	51,459	.47	.26
Unstructured/ Individual	2,303	.20	.11
Unstructured/ Board	3,134	.37	.21
Structured	7,873	.63	.35
Structured/ Board	2,104	.60	.33

how he/she would respond to various situations; (2) job knowledge questions, in which an applicant is assessed as to whether he/she has the basic knowledge necessary to perform the job; (3) job sample–simulation questions, in which mock-ups of job samples or questions utilizing the terminology of the job are used; or (4) worker requirements questions, in which the applicant is asked whether he/she is willing to perform certain tasks under certain working conditions.

The authors focused on structured interviews because of their demonstrated superiority over unstructured interviews. The following three sources of superiority were noted: (1) structured interviews are based on a thorough job analysis; (2) structured interviews assume that an individual's intentions and behaviors are strongly linked; and (3) the use of the same questions with predetermined standards for answers increases the reliability of the interview.

The results indicated that structured interviews correlated with behavioral observation scales and graphic rating scales. For all thirteen studies, a mean uncorrected validity coefficient of .27 was obtained in a total sample size of $N = 870$. No correction for range restriction was performed. When one outlier study was removed and the coefficient was corrected for unreliability, the corrected validity coefficient was .39. The authors concluded that substantial evidence now exists for using structured over unstructured interviewing formats.

A more recent meta-analysis of employment interview validity was conducted by McDaniel, Whetzel, Schmidt, and Maurer (1994). The study included data on more interviews than were available in previous meta-analysis studies. The study also broke down the data into more differentiated analytic categories, such as, situational versus job-related versus psychological interviews, structured versus unstructured interviews, and job performance criterion versus training performance criterion versus tenure criterion. In terms of the number of interview validity studies included in this meta-analysis, this search extending over a period of eight years is perhaps the most complete search ever conducted of interview validities. Analyses are based on 245 coefficients derived from 86,311 individuals.

The interview was analyzed according to its content. The situational interview (behavior intention questions, $N = 946$), the job-related interview ($N = 72,109$), and the psychological interview ($N = 8,376$) were analyzed. For job performance criteria (e.g., performance ratings), situational interviews yield a higher mean validity (.50) than do job-related interviews (.39), which yield a higher mean validity than do psychological interviews (.29).

Structured interviews, regardless of content, are more valid (.44) than unstructured interviews (.33) for predicting job performance criteria. When the content of the interview is job related, structured interviews ($N = 12,847$) are still more valid (.44) than unstructured interviews ($N = 9,330$; .33; job performance criterion). However, when the criterion is training performance, the validity of unstructured and structured interviews is similar (.34 and .36, respectively).

When all interviews are considered together (job performance criterion), individual interviews ($N = 11,393$) appear more valid than board interviews ($N = 11,915$), or .43 versus .32. The individual structured interview ($N = 8,944$) appears to be more valid than the board structured interview ($N = 2,785$), or .46 versus .38. With regard to criteria, interviews are similar in predictive accuracy for job performance (.37) and training performance (.36). Tenure is less predictable by the interview (.20) than are job and training performance.

Huffcutt and Arthur (1994) provide a reanalysis of an early meta-analysis originally performed by Hunter and Hunter (1984). This meta-analysis focused exclusively on entry-level jobs. Hunter and Hunter found that the interview had a mean predictive validity of .14. In their reanalysis Huffcutt and Arthur focused on the following issues: Why were Hunter and Hunter's results different (lower) than more recent meta-analytic reviews? How does interview structure moderate validity of the interview? How much structure is enough structure? Having used a more extensive sample than Hunter and Hunter, Huffcutt and Arthur present mean predictive validity coefficients of .20 (no formal structure), .35 (some formal structure), .56 (high structure with some variability permitted in the interview process) and .57 (high structure, asking all applicants the same questions with no deviation or probing and scoring of each individual response according to benchmark answers). Huffcutt and Arthur conclude that Hunter and Hunter's results were misleading since their sample of interview studies was too small and because they did not consider interview structure in the analysis. The inclusion of structure in the analysis shows that, to a large extent, increasing structure leads to increased validity. However, the implementation of very high structure does not seem to enhance predictive validity to a meaningful degree.

Taken together, the meta-analytic studies show that the structured interview has moderate predictive validity (Nevo and Berman, 1994). Unfortunately, it has not yet been established which features of the structured interview are essential in terms of enhancing the reliability and validity.

RELIABILITY IN EVALUATION OF APPLICANTS

There are several reasons why employment interviews may result in ratings which have low reliability. (An example of low reliability is lack of agreement among raters about the same rating on an applicant, assuming the applicant has performed in the same manner in each interview. Reliability also concerns statistical reliability of ratings. The reader should refer to a text on statistics for more on reliability.) Many interviews have an element of recruiting included. Recruiting requires different means than selection (e.g., presenting a good impression of the organization), and this may reduce the reliability of the evaluation process. There are many sources of interviewer errors (e.g., bias, lack of training, and lack of preparation for the interview) which result in ratings with low reliability. Furthermore, the more unstructured an interview, the less reliable will be the resulting evaluation ratings. For all these reasons (and more) the employment interview has been criticized in the academic literature.

A basic tenet of employee selection research is that a selection procedure cannot be valid if it is not reliable. From the research perspective, validity is the *sine qua non* of selection. Any selection procedure should be demonstrably related to an outcome variable, such as, high performance, low turnover, or advancement. Relationship between the selection procedure and the outcome variables is established by statistical means. It is in the nature of statistical analysis that if one has a predictor (such as an interview evaluation rating) which is not reliable, it reduces the chance of making an accurate prediction using that predictor. The criterion variable also must be reliable for a valid prediction to be made.

Reliability is measured in various ways. In general, a predictor variable is held to be reliable when several raters agree, or when the same rating is obtained in subsequent measurements. A measure is also said to be reliable when it has internal consistency (i.e., its various components are highly interrelated). It has long been assumed that the employment interview has a reliability problem. Research now points the way to improved reliability.

According to Orpen (1985) the typical employment interview has a reliability of .68. According to Wagner (1949) the reliability of 174 sets of ratings he reviewed had a median $r = .57$. Conway, Jako, and Goodman (1995) performed a meta-analysis of interview reliability. They pulled together data from numerous studies, and analyzed 160 reliability coefficients with a total sample size of 20,636 interviews. They found a mean interrater reliability of .70 for the employment interview. Reliabilities for panel interviews (mean = .77) were higher than reliabilities for separate interviews (mean = .53). However, standardizing questions had a stronger moderating effect on reliability when coefficients were from separate (rather than panel) interviews. Multiple ratings were found to be useful when combined mechanically but there was no evidence of usefulness when they were combined subjectively. Based on the reliability data, upper limits of validity were estimated to be .67 for highly structured interviews, .56 for moderately structured interviews, and .34 for unstructured interviews. These upper limits represent the highest validities that could be obtained with a perfectly reliable criterion (observed validities using imperfect criteria tend to be lower).

Ideally in a reliable employment interview process, each applicant would be rated the same if he/she were interviewed over and over again. It would not make a difference if different interviewers conducted the interview. The issue of reliability concerns the ratings, not the person who makes the ratings. One can easily conceive of aspects of the employment interview process which could be modified to improve reliability. A major constraint in modifying the traditional (unstructured) interview format is the acceptability of the revised format to the manager who conducts the interview and the organization's willingness to change the communications climate of the interview. Too much structure may provoke resistance by managers and may appear as mechanistic to job applicants. Some typical methods of improving reliability are the following:

• Ask the same questions of each job applicant
• Use the same schedule of questions for each job applicant
• Provide interviewers with training to make them aware how bias can influence ratings
• Require documentation of why ratings were made
• Provide interviewers with information about various errors that occur in interviews
• Provide role-play training to interviewers to help them become aware of and overcome their errors
• Train interviewers in the use of rating scales and in typical rating errors
• Each applicant should be interviewed by more than one interviewer. A single rating is developed after discussion.
• A board or panel interviews each candidate and a single rating is developed after a discussion

Conclusion

This book offers the practitioner a range of techniques which can be developed into a structured interview process for the employment function. There are some specific recommendations about the basics of the process. There is also coverage of many technical details which the interviewer may choose to add to the basics. The simple cookbook approach of many practitioner interview guides is eschewed in favor of a selection model. The model is to some extent cross-cultural. Multinational firms must take into consideration the fact that U.S. EEO laws and regulations are unique. Some of their restrictions are not relevant in other countries, however their utility should not be overlooked. Much of what is embodied in the equal opportunity laws and regulations is the right thing to do from the standpoint of sound HRM.

The book's focus on competence-based HRM brings an exciting perspective to employment interviewing. The effectiveness of the HRM function is increasingly seen as part of the strategic competence of an organization. Initially, this was based on the increased sophistication of HRM information systems. The computerized HRM information system permits HRM executives to contribute to the strategic planning process in a meaningful way. The advent of competence-based management practices permits another linkage to be formed between HRM and strategic planning. Now each position in the firm can be designed to contribute to the accomplishment of the strategic plan through aligning the position's required competences with the core competence needed by the organization. Furthermore, job applicants can be evaluated as to whether they have the competence necessary to aid the organization in the accomplishment of its strategic objectives. The efficacy of this new way of managing will be borne out by program evaluation studies underway in some leading organizations.

While many organizations have in place sophisticated selection programs, most organizations do not. The investment in time and effort put into the improvement of selection methodology will pay off rapidly for an organization. Too often the best candidate is not hired because there is too much politics, not enough rigor, and inadequate knowledge in the area of employee selection. Individual managers and HRM specialists can contribute to their organization's success by advocating improved employee selection methods. The ideas in this book can be used in such an effort because they will lead to the development of a coherent selection process which can be applied to an entire organization. Methods exist for calculating the cost-effectiveness of selection procedures. Such utility analyses are helpful in explaining to managers the practical benefits of improved selection methodology. The reader can refer to Berman (1993) for an example of utility analysis applied to a selection procedure.

The reader is offered a choice as to how much structure to include in the interview. The traditional conversational interview is the approach with the least structure. The interviewer may choose to utilize the patterned interview. This approach gives the interviewer the chance to follow up on clues the applicant gives as to his/her strengths and weaknesses. The highly structured interview is like a test. It is administered with a great deal of standardization, and the interviewer must carefully follow the predetermined procedures. While limiting the interviewer from following up on hunches, this approach is likely to reduce interviewer errors.

A big payoff for readers of this book will be in the improvement they make in their interviewing skill. The competent interviewer will master the interpersonal communication skills common to many aspects of HRM, namely, employment interviewing, performance reviews, disciplinary interviews, and counseling. Some of the key skills which an interviewer can improve with practice are nonverbal communication, listening, notetaking, empathy, and control.

The competent interviewer will know of and avoid the many pitfalls and potential errors surrounding the interview. Of particular importance is the avoidance of the bias of discrimination. Also important is the self-knowledge which will allow the interviewer to avoid the self-defeating effects of stereotyping, rating errors, and subjective judgment. The competent interviewer will also be aware of the nuances of interviewing error, such as, the contrast effect, the rush to judgment, and first impression errors.

It is important to understand the relevance of the scientific selection model featured in this book for employment interviewing. Interviewers too often settle for a candidate who is not the best person for the job. This may be because of time pressure, lack of adequate recruiting, or insufficient support from the HRM function. The benefits of the scientific selection model in terms of improved performance and lower costs have been amply demonstrated in the research literature. However, to achieve such benefits an organization must be willing to systematically do position analysis, recruiting, multiple interviews, and validation of selection procedures. Also, organizations need to train all personnel who interview job applicants.

With regard to interviewer training, HRM specialists need to know how to take the results of position analysis and develop from them competence factors, interview questions, and rating procedures. Managers who interview must know the basics of interviewing skills. All who interview must be able to do so within the boundaries of Federal and state legislation if they work in the United States. A training program will give interviewers the necessary factual knowledge, a chance to practice their skills, and a chance to receive feedback on their skills.

The material in this book is relevant for both large and small organizations. In the large organization, the HRM function can provide the infrastructure to make such a program happen. In a small organization, it will depend on the willingness and interest of particular managers. If a manager wishes to put into place the principles of competence-based structured interviewing, all the necessary facts are contained within this book. By following the guidelines of this book, a sound program can be implemented by a manager without the help of outside consultants or the HRM function.

SPECIFIC SUGGESTIONS

A number of suggestions are offered for the practitioner. This book provides practitioners the means to implement many improvements in their employment interviewing methodology. The following is a list of some of these improvements:

- Improve recruitment so that there are several applicants for an open position. This will allow use of the selection model of hiring new employees.
- Conduct a critical incident study of a position which must be filled. Develop a competence model for the position based on an analysis of the critical incidents.
- Conduct a job analysis of the open position. Identify the skills, knowledge, and abilities needed to perform on the job.
- Take the following steps to improve the reliability of employment interview evaluation:
  - Use the same schedule of questions for each job applicant
  - Train interviewers in the use of rating scales and in typical rating errors
  - Provide interviewers with training to make them aware how bias can influence ratings
  - Develop rating scales with behavioral anchors indicating varying levels of competence
  - Develop evaluation guides with behavioral examples to assist interviewers in evaluating applicants
  - Conduct interviewer training for all managers who interview; provide written materials about how to interview

- Provide the necessary forms to document how the interview process was conducted; provide interviewers with videotape feedback of the model interviews they perform in training (behavior modeling)

- Certify interviewers in your organization after they have demonstrated the ability to use elements of the competence-based structured interview model. Recertify periodically.

- Do a validation study of the interview process used in the firm. Utilize the EEOC selection guidelines in designing and documenting the study.

- Maintain records of employment data which can be used in subsequent research on the validity of the interview (e.g., ratings on competence factors, performance review ratings, and turnover data).

- Assure that all aspects of the selection process conform to Federal and state guidelines and regulations. Provide training to managers on these guidelines and regulations.

References

Arvey, R. (1979). "Unfair Discrimination in the Employment Interview." *Psychological Bulletin* 86: 736–765.

Arvey, R., and J. Campion. (1982). "The Employment Interview." *Personnel Psychology* 35: 281–322.

Arvey, R., and R. Faley. (1988). *Fairness in Selecting Employees*. Reading, Mass.: Addison Wesley.

ASPA (American Society for Personnel Administration). (1983). *Employee Selection Procedures*. ASPA-BNA Survey No. 45. Washington, D.C.: Bureau of National Affairs.

Bell, A. (1992). *Extraviewing*. Homewood, Ill.: Business One, 72–96.

Berman, J. (1993). "Validation of the P.D.I. Employment Inventory in a Retail Chain." *Journal of Business and Psychology* 7(4): 413–419.

Boyatzis, R. (1982). *The Competent Manager: A Model for Effective Performance*. New York: John Wiley.

Campion, J., and R. Arvey. (1989). "Unfair Discrimination in the Employment Interview." In *The Employment Interview*, ed. R. Eder and G. Ferris. Newbury Park, Calif.: Sage. 61–74.

Campion, M., J. Campion, and P. Hudson. (1994). "Structured Interviewing: A Note on Incremental Validity and Alternative Question Types." *Journal of Applied Psychology* 79(6): 998–1002.

Campion, M., E. Pursell, and B. Brown. (1988). "Structured Interviewing: Raising the Psychometric Properties of the Employment Interview." *Personal Psychology* 41: 25–42.

Campion, M., E. Pursell, and B. Brown. (1991). "Structured Interviewing Techniques for Personnel Selection." In *Applying Psychology in Business*, ed. J. Jones, B. Steffy, and D. Bray. New York: Lexington Books. 251–259.

Cascio, W. (1992). *Managing Human Resources*. New York: McGraw-Hill.

Cava, J. (1995). "Developing Competencies and Organizational Applications." In *Using Competency-Based Tools and Applications to Drive Organizational Performance*. Conference proceedings: 501–527.

Church, A. (1996). "From Both Sides Now: The Employee Interview—the Great Pretender." *TIP: The Industrial Psychologist* 34(1): 108–117.

Conway, J., R. Jako, and D. Goodman. (1995). "A Meta-Analysis of Interrater and Internal Consistency Reliability of Selection Interviews." *Journal of Applied Psychology* 80(5): 565–579.

Cronshaw, S., and W. Weisner. (1989). "The Validity of the Employment Interview." In *The Employment Interview*, ed. R. Eder and G. Ferris. Newbury Park, Calif.: Sage. 269–282.

Dipboye, R. (1989). "Threats to the Increment of Validity of Interview Judgments." In *The Employment Interview,* ed. R. Eder and G. Ferris. Newbury Park, Calif.: Sage. 45–60.

Dipboye, R. (1992). *Selection Interviews: Process Perspectives.* Cincinnati: Southwestern Publishing.

Dipboye, R. (1994). "Structured and Unstructured Selection Interviews: Beyond the Job-Fit Model." *Research in Personnel and Human Resources Management* 12: 79–123.

Dipboye, R., R. Arvey, and D. Terpstra. (1976). "Equal Employment and the Interview." *Personnel Journal* 55: 520–525.

Eder, R., and G. Ferris, eds. (1989). *The Employment Interview*. Newbury Park, Calif.: Sage.

Eder, R., K. Kacmar, and G. Ferris. (1989). "Employment Interview Research: History and Synthesis." In *The Employment Interview*, ed. R. Eder and G. Ferris. Newbury Park, Calif.: Sage.

EEOC (Equal Employment Opportunity Commission). (1978). "Adoption of Four Agencies of Uniform Guidelines on Employee Selection Procedures." Federal Register 43: 38,290–38,315.

Ennis, S., and J. Lawson. (1995). "Utilizing Competencies in Organizational Transformation: Positioning Digital for the Future." In *Using Competency-Based Tools and Applications to Drive Organizational Performance.* Conference Proceedings: 175–205.

Field, H., and R. Gatewood. (1989). "Contextual Effects on Interview Decisions." In *The Employment Interview*, ed. R. Eder and G. Ferris. Newbury Park, Calif.: Sage. 145–157.

Gatewood, R., and H. Field. (1990). *Human Resource Selection.* Chicago: Dryden Press.

Hakel, M. (1970). *Checklists for Describing Job Applicants.* Minnesota: Industrial Relations Center.

Hakel, M. (1982). "Employment Interviewing." In *Personnel Management*, ed. K. Rowland and G. Ferris. Boston: Allyn and Bacon.

Harris, M. (1989). "Reconsidering the Employment Interview." *Personnel Psychology* 42: 691–726.

Hellervik, L. (1977). *Advanced Selection Interviewing Workshop.* Minneapolis: Personnel Decisions, Inc.

Huffcutt, A., and W. Arthur. (1994). "Hunter and Hunter (1984) Revisited: Interview Validity for Entry-Level Jobs." *Journal of Applied Psychology* 79(2): 184–190.

Hunter, J., and R. Hunter. (1984). "Validity and Utility of Alternate Predictors of Job Performance." *Psychological Bulletin* 96: 72–98.

Janz, T. (1989). "The Patterned Behavior Description Interview." In *The Employment Interview*, ed. R. Eder and G. Ferris. Newbury Park, Calif.: Sage. 158–168.

Janz, T., L. Hellervik, and D. Gilmore. (1986). *Behavioral Description Interviewing*. Boston: Allyn and Bacon.

Kirchner, W., and M. Dunnette. (1971). "Identifying the Critical Factors in Successful Salesmanship." In *Readings in Organizational and Industrial Psychology,* ed. G. Yukl and K. Wexley. New York: Oxford University Press. 358–370.

Latham, G. (1989). "The Reliability, Validity, and Practicality of the Situational Interview." In *The Employment Interview*, ed. R. Eder and G. Ferris. Newbury Park, Calif.: Sage. 169–182.

Latham, G., and L. Saari. (1984). "Do People Do What They Say? Further Studies on the Situational Interview." *Journal of Applied Psychology* 69(4): 569–573.

Latham, G., L. Saari, E. Pursell, and M. Campion. (1980). "The Situational Interview." *Journal of Applied Psychology* 65: 431–442.

Lowery, P. (1994). "The Structured Interview: An Alternative to the Assessment Center?" *Public Personnel Management* 23(2): 201–215.

Lunn, T. (1993). "Developing the Talent-Led Company." *Management Development Review* 6(3): 21–23.

Mayfield, E. (1964). "The Selection Interview." *Personnel Psychology* 17: 239–260.

McDaniel, M., D. Whetzel, F. Schmidt, S. Maurer. (1994). "The Validity of Employment Interviews: A Comprehensive Review and Meta-Analysis." *Journal of Applied Psychology* 79: 599–616.

Mirabile, R. (1994). "How to Build a Competency Model: Methods and Issues." *Using Compentecy-Based Tools and Applications to Drive Organizational Performance.* Conference proceedings: 331–347.

Moffat, T. (1979). *Selection Interviewing for Managers.* New York: Harper and Row.

Motowidlo, S., G. Carter, M. Dunnette, N. Tippins, S. Werner, J. Burnett, and M. Vaughan. (1992). "Studies of the Structured Behavior Interview." *Journal of Applied Psychology* 77(5): 571–587.

Nevo, B. and J. Berman. (1994). "The Two-Step Selection Interview: Combining Standardisation with Depth." *Research and Practice in Human Resource Management* 2(1): 89–96.

O'Neal, S., and M. White. (1994). "Designing a Competency Based Compensation System." *Using Compentecy-Based Tools and Applications to Drive Organizational Performance.* Conference proceedings: 141–174.

Orpen, C. (1985). "Patterned Behavior Description Interviews Versus Unstructured Interviews." *Journal of Applied Psychology* 70: 774–776.

Pulakos, E., and N. Schmitt. (1995). "Experience-Based and Situational Interview Questions: Studies of Validity." *Personnel Psychology* 48: 289–308.

Rowe, P. (1989). "Unfavorable Information and Interview Decisions." In *The Employment Interview*, ed. R. Eder and G. Ferris. Newbury Park, Calif.: Sage. 77–89.

Schmitt, N. (1976). "Social and Situational Determinants of Interview Decisions." *Personnel Psychology* 29: 79–101.

Smith, B. (1995). "Developing and Implementing Colgate's New Competency Based Global HR Strategy." *Using Competency-Based Tools and Applications to Drive Organizational Performance.* Conference proceedings: 141–174.

Spenser, L., and S. Spenser. (1993). *Competence at Work: Models for Superior Performance.* New York: John Wiley.

Springbett, B. (1958). "Factors Affecting the Final Decision in the Employment Interview." *Canadian Journal of Psychology* 12: 13–22.

Sternberg, R., and R. Wagner. (1991). "Tacit Knowledge: Its Uses in Identifying, Assessing, and Developing Managerial Talent." In *Applying Psychology in Business:The Manager's Handbook,* ed. J. Jones, B. Steffy, and D. Bray. New York: Human Sciences Press.

Taylor, P., and M. O'Driscoll. (1995). *Structured Employment Interviewing.* Hampshire, U.K.: Gower.

Thornton, G. and W. Byham. (1982). *Assessment Centers and Managerial Performance.* New York: Academic Press.

U. S. Department of Labor. (1972). *Handbook for Analyzing Jobs.* Washington, D.C.: Manpower Administration.

Van Clieaf, M. (1991). "In Search of Competence: Structured Behavior Interviews." *Business Horizons* (March–April): 314–318.

Wagner, R. (1949). "The Selection Interview." *Personnel Psychology* 2: 17–46.

Warmke, D., and D. Weston. (1992). "Success Dispels Myths about Panel Interviewing." *Personnel Journal* (April): 120–126.

Webster, E. (1982). *The Employment Interview: A Social Judgment Process.* Schomberg, Ontario: S.I.P Publications.

Wright, P., P. Lichtenfels, and E. Pursell. (1989). "The Structured Interview: Additional Studies and a Meta-Analysis." *Journal of Occupational Psychology* 62: 191–199.

Subject Index

Name Index

ABOUT THE AUTHOR

JEFFREY A. BERMAN is Associate Professor in the School of Business at Salem State College in Salem, Massachusetts.

He teaches courses in Organizational Behavior and Human Resource Man agement. In addition, Dr. Berman has been affiliated with University of Massachusetts at Boston, Bentley College, and the École Supérieure de Commerce in Tours, France.

He published an article, "Birth of a Black Business," in the *Harvard Business Review* (Sept.–Oct. 1970). Dr. Berman has published numerous other articles based on his research activities. His research has appeared in *The Journal of Business and Psychology*, *The International Journal of Value Based Management*, *The European Journal of Industrial Training*, *Research and Practice in Human Resource Management*, and the *International Journal of Computer Applications and Technology*.

Dr. Berman holds an M.B.A. from Harvard University Graduate School of Business Administration. He holds a Ph.D. from New York University in Industrial/Organizational Psychology. He is a licenced psychologist in the state of Massachusetts.

ISBN 1-56720-050-8

90000>

EAN

9 781567 200508

HARDCOVER BAR CODE